W9-AZV-472

Building Toward Crisis

Saddam Husayn's Strategy for Survival

Amatzia Baram

Policy Paper No. 47

THE WASHINGTON INSTITUTE FOR NEAR EAST POLICY

Published in 1998 in the United States of America by the Washington Institute for Near East Policy, 1828 L Street NW, Suite 1050, Washington, DC 20036

Library of Congress Cataloging-in-Publication Data

Baram, Amatzia, 1938-
    Building Toward Crisis: Saddam Husayn's Strategy for Survival / Amatzia Baram.
        p. cm. — (Policy papers; no. 47)
    Includes bibiliographical references.
    ISBN 0-944029-25-6
    1. Iraq—Politics and government—1979-   2. Iraq—Foreign relations—
1979-   3. Economic sanctions—Iraq. 4. Husayn, Saddam, 1937-   . I. Title.
II. Series: Policy papers (Washington Institute for Near East Policy) ; no. 47.
DS79.7.B349 1998   98-3313
956.7044—dc21   CIP

The Author

Amatzia Baram is an associate professor in the modern history department at Haifa University and a 1998–1999 visiting professor in the government department at Georgetown University. The recipient of The Washington Institute's 1998 Ira Weiner Fellowship, he was a senior fellow at the United States Institute of Peace in 1997–1998.

The author of *Culture, History, and Ideology in the Formation of Ba'thist Iraq: 1968–1989* (St. Martin's, 1991), Dr. Baram coedited (with Barry Rubin) *Iraq's Road to War* (St. Martin's, 1993). He is also the author of more than forty-five articles published in professional magazines, journals, and books.

Dr. Baram received his doctorate in the history of Islamic countries from the Hebrew University, Jerusalem. Before coming to Washington, he was a member of an advisory team on the Middle East for Labor secretary general Ehud Barak.

• • •

Contents

Acknowledgments

I am indebted to The Washington Institute for Near East Policy and its director, Robert Satloff, for their assistance, which made this monograph possible. The Institute's excellent team of research assistants extended to me valuable help in collecting material.

Special thanks go to Kenneth Pollack for his penetrating observations and editing skills. His dedication and expertise added much to this monograph. Thanks are also due to Alan Makovsky, who reviewed the Turkish chapter and opened my eyes to the complexity of Turkish attitudes toward Iraq. Michael Eisenstadt and Robert Satloff likewise scrutinized the book; their comments were extremely helpful. Monica Hertzman's professionalism and attention to detail are also deeply appreciated; it was a great pleasure to work with her on this book.

The last touches of this study, updating it to early 1998, were applied while I was a senior fellow at the United States Institute of Peace. I am grateful to USIP for this, as well as for permitting me to use in this monograph Saddam Husayn's family tree, which I researched and assembled while at the institute in 1997–1998; this family tree appears in a different context in a forthcoming USIP monograph.

Much of the material for this study was gathered with the support of the Israel Science Foundation, a subsidiary of the Israel Academy of Sciences and Humanities, to which I am deeply grateful. Last but not least, my assistants at the University of Haifa—Ronen Zeidel, Navit Ilani, and Eran Arigi—extended invaluable help in collecting material for this monograph. Their intellectual excellence is a rare resource that I was fortunate to be able to tap. I am indebted to them for their enthusiasm and dedication.

• • •

In *Building Toward Crisis,* I refer to the Iraqi president both by his full name, Saddam Husayn, and simply as Saddam; this is for purely technical reasons. Such nomenclature is common in Middle East analysis, both because Husayn is Saddam's father's name, and to prevent confusion with Jordan's King Hussein.

Preface

Saddam Husayn is, regrettably, one of the world's great survivors. He has withstood crushing military defeat, mass insurrection, numerous coup attempts, crippling economic sanctions, and unprecedented international isolation. After nearly a decade of clashes with Saddam, the world is growing weary with the fight, though neither his ambition nor his venality has diminished over time. Yet, if experience is a guide, the combination of an unshackled, economically revitalized Saddam and an international community indifferent to the challenge is a surefire recipe for future confrontation. Having defied United Nations efforts to root out his weapons of mass destruction program for so long, Saddam now seems on a path toward freeing himself from international scrutiny and toward beginning a process of rearmament that will enable him once again to threaten his neighbors—Iranians, Arabs, and Israelis alike—and overall U.S. interests in the Middle East.

In this study, Professor Amatzia Baram, our 1998 Ira Weiner Fellow and one of the world's leading experts on modern Iraq, explains how Saddam has survived. It analyzes the crucial relationship between the Iraqi dictator and the key elements of Iraqi society that have kept him in power for the last two decades: his family, his tribe, the larger confederation of Sunni Arab townsmen from central Iraq, the Ba'th party, and the Iraqi armed forces. It also assesses Iraq's relations with its immediate neighbors and shows how the wider international community actually came to Saddam's rescue over the last two years and offered him a lifeline when his domestic political situation was most precarious.

No one should believe that we have witnessed our last crisis with Saddam. His record is clear—as long as he remains in power, he will challenge America and its allies throughout the Middle East. Understanding how he operates and remains is power, therefore, is the first step toward confronting the challenge he poses.

Mike Stein	Barbi Weinberg
President	Chairman

ix

Executive Summary

Saddam Husayn and Iraq have undergone a remarkable transformation since 1995, when Saddam was fighting for his very survival. Today, Saddam seems firmly in control in Iraq. He has pacified his family and bought time with the tribes, restored some of the Republican Guard's shattered pride, and apparently convinced his power base that his leadership is effective and is progressing toward the goal of ending the sanctions and inspections regimes without having to give up Iraq's WMD arsenal. As long as it is not committed explicitly and decisively to the ouster of the Iraqi president, the international community should not be surprised to see itself further manipulated to suit Saddam Husayn's purposes.

PROBLEMS AT HOME

Although most Western analysts tend to focus on Saddam's strengthened grip on power in Baghdad, the truth is that the regime's domestic support has badly eroded. Today, he must rely on a much smaller group of supporters than ever before to keep himself in power. Indeed, by late 1996, a series of betrayals, failures, and disappointments had left him in a more precarious domestic position than at any time since the desperate moments of March 1991.

By the summer of 1996, Saddam's family was wracked by the defection and return of Saddam's son-in-law, Husayn Kamil, and by an assassination attempt against Saddam's eldest son, 'Udayy. Husayn Kamil had been a trusted lieutenant, and his defection and return to Iraq prompted Saddam to purge the al-Majid wing of his extended family. The assassination attempt left 'Udayy crippled and completed his fall from grace. 'Udayy had driven Husayn Kamil to defect and, as punishment, Saddam had already stripped him of many of his perquisites. The problems in Saddam's family were compounded by frictions within his al-Bu Nasir tribe. By summer 1996, at least five "houses" within the tribe had grievances with Saddam or his family.

Simultaneously, Saddam was wary of signs of fraying solidarity among his other Sunni tribal supporters. Of the five most important Sunni tribes on which Saddam has historically relied, three have fallen under suspicion in recent years. Jubburi tribesmen have remained under suspicion ever since a 1990 plot was uncovered among the Jubbur of the Republican Guard and regular army units. In 1993–1994, military officers of the 'Ubayd also fell under suspicion for coup plotting, while the following year, the al-Bu Nimr of the Dulaym tribe actually revolted against Saddam's rule. Although Jubburis, Ubaydis and Dulaymis all continue to serve in the Republican Guard and other key regime security forces, they have largely been removed from the most sensitive positions of authority and are closely monitored by Saddam's inner circle.

To compensate for the disappointments of his family and the obstreperousness of the tribes, Saddam attempted to revive the Ba'th party as a central executor of his rule. Saddam began reappointing Ba'th party functionaries to positions of responsibility and he began to lean more heavily on the party as an instrument of control and guidance over Iraqi society. Nevertheless, Saddam seems to have decided that the party could not fully become a substitute for family and tribal loyalists. By late 1996, the rehabilitation of the party had appeared to plateau well short of its original prominence.

Meanwhile, the Iraqi armed forces had grown steadily disenchanted with Saddam's leadership. Five years after the Gulf War, the standard of living of regular army personnel remained dismal, and the level of logistical supplies was woeful. This had even begun to affect the Republican Guards, who previously had been protected from the effects of sanctions. The officer corps chafed at the humiliations of the no-fly zones over northern and southern Iraq, the continued Kurdish control over the North, and the frequent reminders that Iraq was powerless to defend itself against the military might of the United States. The weapons inspections were considered a humiliation and the continued sanctions a serious detriment to the national economy and security. Desertions had forced Baghdad to demobilize divisions while mounting maintenance problems had diminished the equipment available to those remaining. These problems had spawned repeated coup attempts from the ranks of the military and the Guard. In March 1995, two regular army brigades suffered severe losses at the hands of Jalal Talabani's Kurds and the Iraq National Congress (INC)

THE TURNING POINT: IRAQ'S ACCEPTANCE OF RESOLUTION 986

These problems reached a boiling point in 1996. That year was a watershed in the post–Gulf War history of Iraq, one that set the stage for the 1997 and 1998 crises.

By the spring of 1996, Saddam's ruinous policies had brought Iraq to the brink of financial crisis. The continuing impact of sanctions with no relief in sight, coupled with the government's efforts to support itself by manipulating currency exchange rates and monetary supplies, had sparked runaway inflation that threatened to cause the total collapse of the Iraqi economy. A similar crisis in 1994 had prompted Saddam to threaten to invade Kuwait, in the hope that this would frighten the UN Security Council into lifting sanctions. This ploy had failed badly, and Saddam was forced to back down lest he provoke a massive U.S. military response. This experience convinced Saddam that he had no alternative: If he was going to prevent the collapse of the Iraqi economy, he had to accept the humiliation of the oil-for-food deal, which he had resisted for so long because he feared it would undermine international pressure to have the sanctions fully lifted.

Almost immediately, another crisis unfolded. In June, his security services uncovered a plot among the Republican Guards to assassinate him. The regime moved quickly and efficiently to snuff out the coup plot, but its mere existence was further proof of growing disaffection even among Saddam's most trusted defenders. Coupled with the painful defeat he suffered in having to accept UN Security Council Resolution 986, it showed Saddam as weak and vulnerable. He needed to find a way to restore the Iraqi military's (and particularly the Guard's) morale and to demonstrate his own strength to his people.

In August, the Kurds provided a way out of his predicament. Months before, Talabani's Patriotic Union of Kurdistan (PUK) had secured some Iranian assistance to launch a large-scale offensive against the rival Kurdish Democratic Party (KDP) of Mas'ud Barzani. Hard-pressed by PUK successes, Barzani turned to Saddam to save the KDP. Saddam consented, and at the end of the month, elements of the Republican Guard attacked the city of Irbil. The Guard smashed the PUK and the nascent organization of the U.S.-backed INC at Irbil. Although American threats prevented Baghdad from conducting additional operations in Iraqi Kurdistan, the seizure of Irbil proved a major victory for Saddam. It simultaneously allowed him to restore the morale of the Republican Guard (and their faith in Saddam himself), to demonstrate that the regime is a major player throughout the country, and to show up the various opposition groups as fractious and impotent. In short, it reversed much of the damage done to his image and his position by the financial crises, the acceptance of 986, and the various military coup attempts.

The events of autumn 1996 provided Saddam's regime with a tremendous boost. His post–Gulf War strategies had brought him much closer to the brink of disaster than many outside of Iraq had realized at the time. Had he not been able to win the great psychological victory at Irbil in August, the humiliation of accepting 986 (because this demonstrated that the hardships he had inflicted on his people for the last five years had only brought Iraq to ruin with nothing to show for the effort) and the growing unrest among the army and the Guard might have seriously undermined his hold on power.

AN UNEXPECTED RESCUER: IRAQ ON THE INTERNATIONAL SCENE

Although Saddam was able to shore up domestic support in 1996, the events of that year merely staved off defeat. They did not indicate that Saddam would somehow be able to prevail in his contest of wills with the United Nations and the United States. In 1997 and 1998, Saddam was able to score important victories which have convinced many that he will ultimately prevail.

What is most unusual about these events is that external factors have been Saddam's greatest boon, opening up new opportunities for Iraqi policies and helping to ameliorate Saddam's domestic problems. External pressures have always played a role in Iraqi decision making, but traditionally their impact has been modest or episodic. Iraqi Ba'thi politics, especially under Saddam, have proven highly insular. The Iraqi president has made policy primarily based on the requirements of Iraq's domestic milieu.

To the extent that external affairs shaped Baghdad's decision making, Iraq's immediate neighbors have had the greatest impact. These countries, however, have not been the source of the regime's renewed lease on life.

- The brightest regional spot for Baghdad was, surprisingly, **Syria**, which shifted from extreme hostility to a guarded reconciliation. The budding Israeli–Turkish relationship and the stalemate in Syrian–Israeli negotiations prompted Hafiz al-Asad to cast about for allies and, finding none, he decided to extend a slim olive branch to Saddam Husayn. Thus during 1997 and early 1998 there was a flurry of activity between Damascus and Baghdad. Nevertheless, the exchanges were relatively minor, and Damascus made clear to Baghdad that, for now, their "amity" would not extend to anything more meaningful than limited economic and diplomatic ties.
- Iraqi relations with **Iran** have improved only marginally. In 1998, the two sides exchanged prisoners of war. Nevertheless, Tehran and Baghdad remained mired in a range of problems stemming from the end of their eight-year war. While bemoaning American "hegemony" in its propaganda, Iran seems delighted by Iraq's continued containment and forced disarmament at the hands of the UN. Moreover, upon taking over the Iranian presidency in August 1997, Muhammad Khatemi has sought improved relations with the United States and Saudi Arabia—to Iraq's detriment. Further improvements in Iraqi–Iranian relations are possible but will happen only slowly and incrementally, if at all.
- **Turkey** has continued to be a frustration for Baghdad. On the one

hand, Ankara unquestionably would like to see UN sanctions lifted because it too has suffered from the cut-off of trade and oil-transshipment revenues from Iraq. Likewise, many Turks would probably like to see Iraqi regime forces in complete control of Kurdistan in the hope that Baghdad would stamp out terrorism by the Kurdistan Workers' Party (PKK) from the Iraqi side of their border. On the other hand, the generals who stand behind the Turkish government have made clear their commitment to the United States and their insistence that Ankara cooperate with Washington on the question of Iraq.

- Meanwhile, **Jordan** has steadily distanced itself from Iraq in favor of closer relations with the United States and Israel. After Husayn Kamil's defection, King Hussein went so far as to publicly embrace the notion of supporting opposition to Saddam's regime. Nevertheless, Jordan still depends on Iraq for cheap oil, and many in Amman still see Iraq as a lucrative market for Jordanian goods. The Islamists, on the other hand, support Saddam for ideological reasons. Jordanian support for the Iraqi opposition therefore appears to have dissipated.

- Iraq is now trying to convince **Kuwait** to improve bilateral relations and to cease its opposition to Iraq's rehabilitation. These blandishments are usually accompanied with Iraqi threats, though, which only hardens the emirate in its determination to oppose the Iraqi regime.

- Finally, Iraq has also sought a reconciliation with **Saudi Arabia**. Like the Kuwaitis, the Saudis have not been convinced, and they remain staunchly committed to the containment and disarmament of Iraq. Even so, the Saudis have moved to improve relations with Iran as a balance to Iraq should the United States prove unable to live up to all of its commitments. Saudi reservations regarding military action against Iraq are the combined result of domestic constraints and closer ties with Syria and Egypt.

Instead of its immediate neighbors, it was the more far off world that came to Saddam's rescue in 1996–1998. The intervention of France, Russia, China, and more distant Arab countries (e.g., Egypt), brought tremendous pressure on the UN and the chief backers of strict containment, principally the United States and Britain. The success of Iraqi propaganda in convincing Western and Arab publics that lifting sanctions is the only way to alleviate the suffering of the Iraqi people created a sense that Washington, rather than Baghdad, was increasingly isolated.

Although Iraq was forced to beat tactical retreats in the crises of October–November 1997 and January–February 1998, Saddam essentially succeeded in winning important concessions on a range of issues related to weapons inspections. To the Iraqi people—and most important of all, to Saddam's power base—these concessions suggested that time was working in Saddam's favor and that his strategy of confrontation was succeeding. These were critical victories for Saddam. As long as his supporters found it hard to see any light at the end of the sanctions tunnel, they were restless, unhappy, and willing to consider moving against him. The proof was in the assassination attempts, tribal dissension, and other signs that Saddam's base of power was narrowing. Today, the crises Baghdad initiated with the UN have begun to make both Saddam's followers and opponents believe that he may just prevail after all.

CONCLUSIONS: DRAGONS AHEAD

Saddam Husayn has discovered that international crises can prove helpful in strengthening his grip on power inside Iraq. Saddam's recent string of qualified foreign policy successes allowed him to stunt the growth of the domestic challenges to his rule. Given Saddam's track record, it is likely that he will continue to pursue this course as long as he believes it to be successful.

For Saddam, "success" primarily means strengthening his domestic position—even if at the expense of his international position. Western efforts to deal with Saddam during the periodic crises he creates must start from this perspective. The most damaging outcome of any crisis for Saddam would be one that proved him a failure as a leader. At least four events or developments could each lead his power base to such a conclusion:

- If Saddam's actions were to provoke the West to conduct a powerful, sustained military campaign that destroyed important elements of his military power;
- If he could not demonstrate to his power base that he will soon be able to bring to an end the UN inspections regime and with it the oil embargo;
- If he were unable to retain any of Iraq's WMD arsenal; or
- If he were to lose the propaganda campaign he has waged within Iraq.

To prevent the first three, then, Saddam must continue to push hard to show his supporters the "light at the end of the tunnel" and so remove the domestic threat that still looms over his rule. To that end, Saddam must keep the French and Russians on his side, in particular. The combination of a breach with them and an American air campaign may leave him badly bruised both militarily and politically. Without France and Russia, most Arabs too may forsake him. As for the propaganda campaign, the United States and the UN can combat it by restructuring the oil-for-food arrangements to include medicines and infrastructure projects that could provide purified water, sewage treatment, and adequate electricity.

xvi

Chapter 1

Introduction

In the autumn of 1997 Saddam Husayn launched a new confrontation against the United Nations Special Commission on Iraq (UNSCOM). Although Iraqi efforts to hamper the work of the UN inspectors were nothing new, this time there were important differences. After a series of weak responses from the Security Council, Saddam escalated the confrontation one step further by announcing that Iraq would no longer allow Americans to participate in the inspections. In late November, Saddam retracted this demand when Russia and France convinced him that he was undermining their efforts to see the international sanctions on Iraq removed. But then on January 17, 1998, Saddam pushed the crisis to an even higher level of tension by issuing an ultimatum to the United Nations: Lift the sanctions by May 20, 1998, or else Iraq would cease all cooperation with UNSCOM.

Although, as will be shown below, Iraq had clearly been building toward this confrontation for several years, Saddam's belligerence and determination to challenge the heart of the UN sanctions regime were unprecedented. What led Baghdad to this new, far more aggressive, and risky course of action? There is much evidence that one important aspect of Saddam's thinking was the international political context. In the first half of 1997, Saddam saw a combination of threats and opportunities in the international environment that led him to his decision. On the one hand, the new UNSCOM chief, Ambassador Richard Butler of Australia, promised to be as tough as, or tougher than, his predecessor, Ambassador Rolf Ekeus of Sweden. Butler's first report to the Security Council criticized Iraq for its failure to cooperate with UNSCOM and its failure to comply with the terms of the ceasefire agreement—suggesting to Saddam that he was unlikely to get a "clean bill of health" from UNSCOM anytime soon. On the other hand, the international coalition that the United States had forged after Iraq's invasion of Kuwait was clearly eroding. France and Russia had made it clear to Baghdad that they wanted an end to the sanctions so they could resume their lucrative commercial relations with Iraq. Syria was in favor of Iraq's rehabilitation, and some other Arab states showed far less commitment to the UN-imposed embargo than ever before, each for their own reasons. The international media focused on the (very real) plight of average Iraqis under the UN sanctions but, in so doing, uncritically echoed Baghdad's unreliable statistics of death and illness from the the embargo. Other countries simply seemed less compelled by the need to contain Saddam, and U.S. and British diplomacy found itself in an unprecedently difficult position. The UN Security Council regularly ignored Iraqi transgressions, and despite U.S. and British efforts to the contrary, its rebukes grew weaker and weaker over time. As could only be expected, this convergence of forces weighed heavily in Saddam's decision to inaugurate a crisis intended to destroy the entire UN program of sanctions or, at least, deal it a major blow.

The above account ignores two aspects that are in fact generally overlooked. First, the years 1995 to 1997 were the first time since the early 1970s that Saddam Husayn's power base showed meaningful cracks. Moreover, 1997 was the first time since the mid-1970s that, Saddam relied as heavily on Iraq's "far abroad"—the superpowers—as on his domestic power base, and least of all on Iraq's neighbors. In 1974–1976, Saddam reshaped Iraq's foreign relations, directing them toward a phase of cooperation with most of his close neighbors—Iran, the Gulf states, Jordan, and Turkey. Since that time, he has consistently turned for help first to his domestic power base, then to this "near abroad." Since 1997, however, he has been pinning his hopes mainly on Russia, France, and China.

Saddam has officially held power in Iraq since 1979—and he was effectively the power behind President Ahmad Hasan al-Bakr since the early 1970s—mainly because he gives clear priority to domestic considerations over foreign policy issues. Throughout his career as chief of internal security (1968–1979), then president, whenever Iraq's foreign interests clashed with perceived domestic security interests, the latter always prevailed. Insofar as internal security is concerned, Saddam Husayn has never taken any chances. The result was that, while Iraq's relations with the world's superpowers often suffered, Saddam's control over the domestic scene remained near total. Thus, for example, between 1968 and 1971 he cracked down harshly on the communist party of Iraq, even though this soured his relations with Moscow and slowed military weapons transfers—this at a time when he had a brewing confrontation with Iran over the Shatt al-Arab. Likewise, it was mainly (though not exclusively) his fear of threats to the Ba'th regime, in the form of domestic unrest—a Kurdish revolt the regime was unable to suppress, and Shi'i civil strife—that forced him to sign the March 1975 agreement with the Shah of Iran in which he conceded Iraqi sovereignty over parts of the Shatt al-Arab. It was again the fear of communist ascendancy in Iraq that pushed Saddam to crack down on the communists in 1978–1979 and to denounce the Soviet invasion of Afghanistan at the end of 1979, even though he badly needed Soviet military aid against Ayatollah Ruhollah Khomeini's Iran.

During the Iraq–Iran War, as before, he relied primarily on his sturdy domestic power base; secondarily on Gulf Arabs, Jordan, and Egypt; and finally on his relations with the far abroad. Indeed, Saddam survived in times of great danger to Iraq or to his rule—or both—because he knew how to support his domestic policies by developing his foreign relations, first with the near abroad and then the far abroad. Thus, during the Iraq–Iran War, there were no reports of meaningful attempts at a coup d'etat by military personnel, the party, or the various internal security apparati, and neither were there any reported cases of a popular uprising against the regime, even in the Shi'i South. The reasons for this domestic calm were many, but mainly they were fear of the regime's effective internal security apparati, which were certain to respond with great ferocity; fear of Iranian occupation, common even amongst many Shi'i Arab Iraqis; and, last but not least, the fact that the regime managed to preserve a fairly high standard of living and supply its armed forces with all they needed to conduct modern, large-scale warfare. This prevented food riots, kept the soldiers in their trenches, and secured the loyalty of the army officer's corp. All this could not have been achieved without Saddam's policy of keeping most Arab regimes on his side and convincing the superpowers and Europe that supporting him was in their interest. Without Gulf Arab money, Egyptian workers, and Gulf and Jordanian supply routes, Iraq may have been been crushed under the weight of the repeated Iranian offensives. Soviet and French arms supplies depended on these routes, and it is doubtful whether they would have extended credits to Iraq without the assurance of Arab support. Indeed, even with this support, in January 1987, when the last major Iranian offensive was at its zenith, France was apparently considering dropping support for Iraq.[1]

Between 1990 and 1996, Saddam's Iraq was denied such Arab and international support. Although Iraq was no longer fighting a major shooting war after February 1991, political isolation and the international oil and weapons embargo greatly tested Saddam's hold in the domestic arena. Economic, social, and political pressures produced, for the first time since 1973, major fissures in Saddam's power base. These pressures started with a military defeat of Iraqi regular forces by a Kurdish militia near Irbil in March 1995 and continued with a bloody confrontation between factions of Saddam's extended family, which led to the defection, return, and murder of Saddam's son-in-law, Gen. Husayn Kamil; the discovery of several dangerous coup plots in the innermost circles of Saddam's security apparatus; increased tension between Saddam and some of his most important tribal supporters; grave economic problems that forced Iraq to accept UN Security Council Resolution 986 (the oil-for-food deal); and an attack on Saddam's eldest son, 'Udayy, which left him seriously wounded. Even though the Iraqi president has managed to ride all the storms, toward the autumn of 1996 his power base was less supportive than at any time since the early 1970s. His inability to combine a firm hold on the domestic scene with lavish oil revenues or, alternatively, with Arab support and international assistance, as he had done during the 1980s, produced very ominous portents inside Iraq. To diffuse the threat, the Iraqi leader had to make a choice: Either make further concessions to the UN—as he did between 1991 and 1996, when he had no support from abroad—or initiate a series of confrontations with the UN in the hope that he could erode the international oil embargo. Yet, making further and meaningful concessions—such as revealing, at long last, all his weapons of mass destruction—could either lead to the end of the embargo or to the loss of support from his power base, or both. Moreover, confronting a unified international coalition could lead to another military disaster and thus loss of power. At that point, ironically, the far abroad and, to a lesser extent, near abroad came to his aid.

Saddam's survival in 1997 depended, in the first place, on support from Russia, France, and China, and for various reasons, such support was forthcoming. For Saddam, this was a reversal of the usual order of things. The Arabs were still less than supportive, but Saddam's decision to confront rather than to concede was made under the impression that, while his traditional second line of defense—the Arab front—was still lukewarm, his far abroad was becoming increasingly supportive and could be manipulated to his advantage. Thus it was that Saddam Husayn regained, to a large extent, his hold over his power base.

This book endeavors to analyze two of the three concentric circles discussed above. It starts with the various components of Saddam's power base—from the extended family, through the tribe and the coalition of tribes that Saddam managed to forge, to the ruling Ba'th party, the army, and very briefly, the Republican and Special Republican Guards. It then discusses the fissures within these power bases and evaluates them in terms of regime survival. The book then turns to Saddam's near abroad, specifically Iraq's closest neighbors. For reasons of practicality, Iraq's relations with its far abroad—the superpowers—are discussed in this study only in passing, but the outcome of the change of heart in Paris, Moscow, and Beijing is an integral part of this study.

NOTE

1   An interview with French officials, January 1987.

Chapter 2

Family and Tribe: Saddam's Shrinking Power Base

By late 1996, Saddam Husayn faced serious problems at home. After the Gulf War, he had increasingly vested power in his own family and a handful of Sunni Arab tribes, believing them the only elements in the Iraqi state he could trust. This shift became necessary when other elements of the Iraqi state upon whom Saddam had relied at one time or another had fallen into disfavor. The members of his Ba'th party had proven themselves unenthusiastic—and often incompetent—during and following the Gulf War. For its part, the Iraqi Army was thoroughly humiliated by its defeat in Kuwait, and Saddam feared that demoralization could easily turn to disaffection. Thus, by late 1991, only his tribal allies and relatives and the military units in which they are paramount remained trusted. Yet, within only a few years, even these groups began to disappoint Saddam. In March 1995, Iraqi regular army units were defeated by Jalal Talabani's Kurds and the Iraq National Congress (INC) in the North. Between 1990 and 1995, three of the most important Sunni tribes on whom Saddam relied were implicated in coup attempts. Saddam's family proved venal, fractious, and difficult for the president to control, leading to a series of scandals that seriously tarnished his honor and his image, and led him to question the value of his relatives as state servants. His tribe, too, started showing signs of strain, and in the Republican and Special Republican Guards, Saddam discovered signs of disaffection.

Even though 1997 saw some improvements, the situation remained precarious. These problems were therefore the crucial first elements of

Saddam's decision to challenge the United Nations (UN). They signaled a dramatic erosion in Saddam's power base by demonstrating to the Iraqi leader that each of the pillars that he had previously used to buttress his regime—the army, the party, the Sunni tribes, his own tribe, and his family—were growing weaker. It was this narrowing of Saddam's power base, and the fears of a coup it conjured in his mind, that forced Saddam to cast about for means to restore his internal position. Thus, understanding Saddam's decision to take on the UN sanctions regime requires understanding the domestic events that led him to this course of action.

THE DEFECTION OF HUSAYN KAMIL

In August 1995, Saddam Husayn's two sons-in-law, Husayn and Saddam Kamil Hasan al-Majid, along with a third brother and several cousins, defected to Jordan. Until then, Husayn Kamil had been one of Saddam's most powerful henchmen, overseeing Iraq's military industry, including its nonconventional weapons programs and a host of other responsibilities. The fear that the defectors would divulge crucial information about Iraq's nonconventional weapons holdings, and thus expose Iraq to the wrath of the UN, created a panic in Baghdad. It prompted Saddam unexpectedly to turn over a million pages of documents and numerous videotapes containing a wealth of information about Iraq's missile, chemical, nuclear, and biological weapons programs to the UN Special Commission on Iraq (UNSCOM). Most striking was the revelation that—contrary to its own previous assertions—Iraq had produced massive quatities of anthrax, botulinum toxin, and other lethal biological agents. At that time, UNSCOM had been moving closer to providing Iraq with a "clean bill of health" over its missile and chemical weapons capabilities, but these revelations convinced UNSCOM chief Rolf Ekeus of Iraq's perfidy. Baghdad's hope that the UN oil embargo would be lifted quickly evaporated.[1]

In addition to the damage to Iraq's international standing, the defections were a major blow to Saddam's psyche and his domestic standing. They brought to light new problems within Saddam's own family, further diminishing the number of loyal relatives Saddam could count on to occupy key government and military posts and leaving Saddam fearful that potential rivals might believe him to be weakened and vulnerable. In addition to their marital ties, both Husayn Kamil and his brother were also second cousins of the president on his father's side—the most important family tie in Iraqi society. To add insult to injury, they took their wives

(Saddam's daughters) and their children (Saddam's grandchildren) with them. This was particularly humiliating for the president, because in Arab–Islamic societies a woman owes her first allegiance to her father rather than to her husband: A man can divorce his wife with relative ease in the Islamic tradition, so a woman must always make sure that she can go back to her father's family if she is divorced. By defecting with their husbands from their father's domain, Saddam's daughters humiliated him. This was particularly painful for a man obsessed with honor and who had habitually presented himself as a model "family man."

The fact that Husayn Kamil was not only a blood relation, but a young man whom the president had promoted at break-neck speed (he rose from second lieutenant in 1980 to lieutenant general, chief of Iraq's military industries, and defense minister by 1991) was a further insult. Saddam had always cultivated an image of omniscience, especially when it came to picking his lieutenants. Likewise, in several programmatic speeches he condoned nepotism, explaining that Moses also resorted to such practices.[2] Saddam admitted afterwards that the Kamils' defection "hurt it [the family] mentally, . . . hurt it very deeply."[3]

As distinct from its international repercussions, the defection of the Kamils caused minimal damage to the regime at home. Demonstrating his usual mastery of Iraqi domestic politics, Saddam managed to cut his losses in a way that appears to have been very effective. His most important action was to announce that, unless they had been directly involved in the defection, Iraqis who had worked with Husayn Kamil had nothing to worry about. The Ministry of Interior declared only the defectors themselves to be "traitors": Husayn and Saddam Kamil, their brother Hakim Kamil, and their cousins, the brothers 'Izz al-Din and Jasim Muhammad Hasan (Jasim eventually returned to Baghdad and it is not clear whether a third brother, Ibrahim, joined the defectors). Kamil Hasan al-Majid, the defectors' father, was not touched after his sons had fled, but he was ostracized socially.[4]

Within Saddam's family, other segments of the Hasan al-Majid branch dissociated themselves from the defectors by authorizing anyone to spill the blood of Husayn Kamil and the other defectors with impunity. In Iraq, this is called *hadr al-dam* (permission to spill blood), or *al-tabarru* (to disown).[5] According to traditional tribal norms, "exposing" the renegade to the wrath of other tribal units is the furthest the *khams*—the five-generation unit within which every adult male is responsible for avenging the blood and honor of any member in the unit—can go against one of its own members. By so doing, the rest of Saddam's paternal family cleansed themselves of the stains of the defections and could therefore still be of use to the president. Indeed, despite the defection, a few of them remained in very prominent positions in the regime's internal security apparatus. For example, Saddam's first cousin 'Ali Hasan al-Majid remained his cousin's chief troubleshooter: In 1995 he was placed in charge of all party branches in a large section of Baghdad, and in the summer of 1997 he was reportedly moved to the Shi'i south (Basra and Nasiriyya) to suppress the restless population there.[6] 'Ali's brother, 'Abd al-Hasan al-Majid, retained his senior position in General Intelligence. Likewise, Shabib Sulayman al-Majid retained his position as a *murafiq* (escort) of the president, Rukkan 'Abd al-Ghaffur Sulayman al-Majid Razzuqi held on to his job as *al-Murafiq al-Aqdam* (Saddam's chief bodyguard), and Kamal Mustafa 'Abd Allah al-Sultan continued to serve as chief of staff of the Republican Guard.[7]

Saddam also moved to reduce the risk of another family crisis by dealing with what some believed was the reason for Husayn Kamil's flight. One of the first things he did after the defection was to demote and publicly humiliate his eldest son, 'Udayy. To start with, he torched 'Udayy's collection of vintage cars.[8] 'Udayy received a public slap in the face from the foreign minister, who stated that 'Udayy was only an athlete and not, as some outside Iraq believed, his father's heir apparent. This was because, as the foreign minister said, "He is not in a position [read: fit] to govern."[9] 'Udayy is still chairman of Iraq's Olympic committee, in which capacity he was further embarrassed when an Iraqi athlete defected in the 1996 Atlanta Olympic games; he still runs his private newspaper, *Babil*, which was first published in March 1991;[10] and he also has a monthly magazine, *al-Rafidayn* (Mesopotamia), and a TV station, *Sawt al-Shabbab min Dar al-Salam* (The Voice of Youth from the Abode of Peace). His high profile as de facto minister of youth[11] was dealt a major blow, however: In late 1995 he was still chairman of the executive committee of the Student Association, but he lost his position as president of the General Union of Iraqi Youth, to which he had been "elected" on April 24, 1994.[12] 'Udayy also lost much of his control over Iraqi media and cultural affairs, and he was stripped of his two most powerful positions within Saddam's security apparatus.[13] First, he was deprived of his position as head of "Operation Call of the Leader," a nationwide effort launched in March 1995 to repair Iraq's mushrooming fleet of rusting and inoperable weaponry. Second,

'Udayy was forced to surrender command of Saddam's *Fida'iyyin*, a new militia that had given him, at long last, his own private army.[14] The Fida'iyyin were given to a distant relative, but this time a professional officer, Lt. Gen. Muzahim Sa'b Hasan, former commander of the Iraqi Air Force.[15] Finally, Saddam elevated 'Udayy's more stable brother, Qusayy, to the position of the regime's foremost security personality.[16]

Saddam's dramatic punishment of 'Udayy lends credence to reports from many sources that 'Udayy was largely to blame for Husayn Kamil's defection. Indeed, King Hussein disclosed to an Israeli reporter that "As far as we know, this was a family crisis, in the personal context, for a fairly long period."[17] Jordanian foreign minister 'Abd al-Karim al-Kabariti admitted that a serious case of "family quarrel" was involved.[18] According to these reports, when Husayn Kamil was recuperating from brain surgery in Amman in mid-February 1994, 'Udayy quietly incorporated into his economic empire parts of Kamil's military procurement network.[19] These assets are a rich source of kickbacks, and Kamil relied on them to provide for his entourage. Upon returning to Baghdad, Kamil was reportedly incensed upon learning of 'Udayy's depradations. Likewise, Operation Call of the Leader—which 'Udayy launched only a few weeks later—also threatened to bring another large aspect of Kamil's military industrialization empire under 'Udayy's control.[20] When confronted by Husayn Kamil, 'Udayy reportedly threatened him with a trial that would expose rampant corruption in the defense industries, and he even threatened to kill him— hardly an idle threat given 'Udayy's bloody record.[21] Barzan Ibrahim, the president's half brother and Iraq's ambassador to the UN in Geneva, implied such trouble in an interview with *al-Hayat*. Barzan lashed out against 'Udayy and Kamil alike, describing both as "greedy, unfit for power," and even against Saddam, by stating that the way in which his half-brother chose his heirs was "unacceptable."[22]

These bitter words should be seen against the background of a three-way conflict within the family involving Saddam's sons, his paternal cousins the Majids, and his half-brothers the Ibrahims. (The Ibrahims belong, through their father, to another branch of the tribe, 'Umar Bek al-Thalith). This family rivalry surfaced, for the first time, after the death of the president's mother, Sabha Talfah al-Masallat, in 1982. As long as she was alive, Saddam Husayn had to consider her views over all family matters. Yet, once she was out of the picture he began making arbitrary decisions that were bound to create tensions. In late 1983 he broke his promise to marry his elder daughter Raghad to Barzan's son and instead married her to Husayn Kamil, his paternal second cousin once removed. Barzan protested and was ousted from his position as director general of Iraqi General Intelligence (in charge of most cloak-and-dagger activities abroad) and sent to manage a chicken farm. His younger brother, Sib'awi Ibrahim, resigned in protest or was dismissed from his position as deputy director of General Security (*al-Amn al-'Amm*), the largest domestic security organization. In 1989 Sib'awi was reinstated, and two years later another brother, Watban Ibrahim Hasan, was made minister of the interior. Yet, during the years that the Ibrahims were out of Saddam's favor, the Majids usurped their previous prominence and power.

Perhaps inevitably, the rancor between the Ibrahims and the Majids drew in 'Udayy, who saw an opportunity to increase his own power by dividing and conquering. Almost from the moment Watban took office as interior minister, 'Udayy used his newspaper and TV station to attack the performance of his uncle. 'Udayy's constant attacks were a major factor in Watban's eventual ouster in May 1995. But having his uncle sacked was not enough for 'Udayy, and the night before the Kamils' defection a row broke out during which 'Udayy shot Watban, wounding him seriously in the leg. When Iraqi TV later interviewed Watban, he claimed his injured leg and the wounds of two of his companions were the results of "an unfortunate accident," the nature of which he would not disclose. To dispel rumors that his son, Ahmad, had been killed, Watban assured the viewers that Ahmad had not been with him when the accident occurred. Then, to dispel reports that he and his aides were shot by 'Udayy, he declared that "the family's unity is stronger than ever." 'Udayy's *Babil* described Watban's injury as the result of an accidental "jubilation" shooting.[23] Seen from 'Udayy's viewpoint it was, indeed, a mere accident that Watban had survived, and it may be that shooting his uncle was a kind of jubilee for 'Udayy, but there is little doubt that he was the perpetrator.[24]

The infighting among 'Udayy, the Majids, and the Ibrahims culminated with Husayn Kamil's defection, which prompted Saddam finally to discipline his unruly family. In addition to stripping 'Udayy of his more important titles, the president removed many other close relatives from senior posts. For example, after being dismissed from the Interior Ministry in May 1995, Watban Ibrahim was appointed to the meaningless position of adviser to the president and was replaced by a senior party old-timer. Meanwhile, Watban's brother Sib'awi Ibrahim was again dismissed from the powerful post of director of General Security soon after Husayn Kamil's defection.[25] Finally, the eldest Ibrahim brother, Barzan, remains in virtual exile in Geneva. Thus Qusayy Saddam Husayn, alone among the family, remained unchallenged as his father's chief lieutenant. But then, even he is under the supervision of someone who is not a member of the extended family: Lt. Gen. 'Abd al-Hamid Humud of the internal security forces.

These punishments hardly ended the three-way family feud, however. Barzan's interview in *al-Hayat* revealed that his side of the family remains extremely bitter: Not only did they lose all of their powerful and profitable positions, but Watban was badly wounded and 'Udayy—the chief culprit—was not held accountable. For their part, the Kamils too undoubtedly feel themselves ill-treated by 'Udayy and have lost their cherished position of superiority over the Ibrahims. Husayn and Saddam Kamil had been two of the most powerful of the Kamils, especially since their uncle 'Ali Hassan al-Majid had been relieved as minister of defense only a short time before. With their departure, the Kamils suddenly found themselves bereft of much of the prestige and clout they had previously enjoyed. These various grudges were then exacerbated by the next episode in the family drama.

In February 1996, in a stunning turnabout, Husayn Kamil and his family suddenly returned to Iraq. On the border, the men were immediately separated from Saddam's daughters and the children. Although Saddam had publicly pardoned them, the next night Husayn Kamil, both of his brothers, their father, possibly two sisters, and their families were slaughtered in the home of a relative. The details of the assassination of the Kamil brothers are not clear. According to the official version, the offspring of Saddam's paternal great-grandfather, 'Abd al-Ghaffur, ganged up on the defectors and their father, Kamil Hassan, and killed them at one of the family's homes in a gun battle to redeem the family's honor. Even though Saddam had granted the Kamils amnesty, he pointed out that "the family" had its own, fully justified, agenda: "Had it not responded to the deep shame inflicted on it," he explained, "then [any one] would have had the right to stone its [the family's] sons."[26] These murders bear mute testimony to the humiliation Saddam harbored from their defection.

The most remarkable fact about the assassination was that the members of the hit team were carefully chosen to represent the five generations of Saddam's khams. It requires some detective work and a close reading of Saddam's family tree to decipher the identity of the assassins. Saddam's

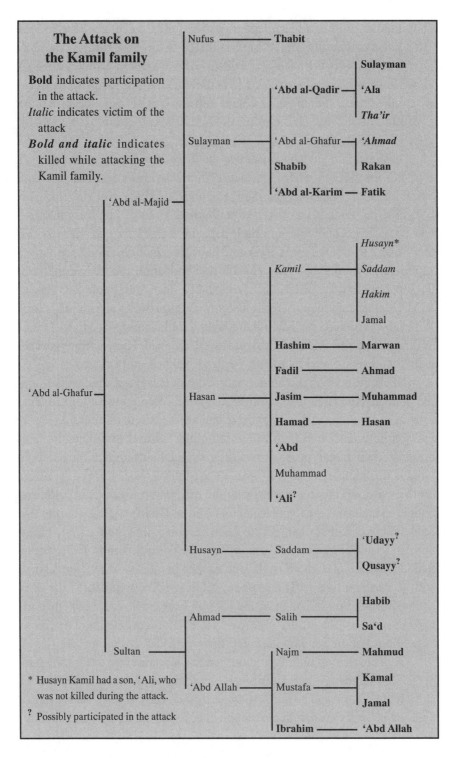

The Attack on the Kamil family

Bold indicates participation in the attack.
Italic indicates victim of the attack
Bold and italic indicates killed while attacking the Kamil family.

Nufus —— **Thabit**

'Abd al-Majid —

'Abd al-Ghafur —

Sulayman ——

'Abd al-Qadir —— Sulayman / 'Ala / *Tha'ir*

'Abd al-Ghafur —— *'Ahmad*

Shabib —— Rakan

'Abd al-Karim —— Fatik

Kamil —— *Husayn** / *Saddam* / *Hakim* / Jamal

Hasan ——
Hashim —— **Marwan**
Fadil —— **Ahmad**
Jasim —— **Muhammad**
Hamad —— **Hasan**
'Abd
Muhammad
'Ali?

Husayn —— Saddam —— 'Udayy? / Qusayy?

Sultan ——

Ahmad —— Salih —— Habib / Sa'd

Najm —— **Mahmud**

'Abd Allah —— Mustafa —— **Kamal** / **Jamal**

Ibrahim —— 'Abd Allah

* Husayn Kamil had a son, 'Ali, who was not killed during the attack.

? Possibly participated in the attack

great-grandfather, 'Abd al-Ghaffur, had two sons: Sultan and 'Abd al-Majid.[27] The regime reported that the offspring of both Sultan and 'Abd al-Majid were involved (Saddam himself belongs to 'Abd al-Majid's branch). Sultan had two sons, Ahmad and 'Abd Allah. If they were alive in February 1996, they would still have been far too old to participate in a gun battle, but 'Abd Allah's offspring unquestionably did participate. These offspring included five sons, the eldest being Ibrahim and Mustafa. Ibrahim and two of his nephews, 'Abd Allah Mustafa and Maj. Gen. Kamal Mustafa (commander of the Special Republican Guard), also participated, and there were two other Sultans involved. On the Majid side there were no less than sixteen men involved in the murder. Among them were all of Husayn Kamil's paternal uncles except 'Ali Hasan al-Majid, whose name was not mentioned in the regime's reporting, and Muhammad Hasan al-Majid, whose son 'Izz al-Din had defected with Husayn Kamil to Jordan.[28] Yet, according to opposition sources, 'Ali Hasan al-Majid, 'Udayy, and Qusayy, were actually the moving forces behind the murder.[29] If true, their names were probably dropped from the list so as not to involve the party and the president's nuclear family in the murder. All of Husayn Kamil's uncles were accompanied by their sons. Finally, there were several other Majids as well, most conspicuously Rukan 'Abd al-Ghaffur Sulayman al-Majid (Razzuqi), the president's chief companion and bodyguard.[30]

There is little doubt that the murder was performed on the direct orders of the president. But his intention apparently was that the blood would be on the hands of those who did the killing and took responsibility for it. It is highly significant that Saddam made sure that five generations of his family would be involved in the murder, as this is the canonical structure of a tribal khams. Saddam perverted the tribal code, though, because traditionally a khams never turns against its own members. The most it does is dissociate itself from a renegade by excommunicating him, thereby permitting his enemies to kill him. The khams itself never does the killing. Indeed, in most circumstances, the khams will make an intense effort to resolve blood feuds within the khams through negotiations and compensation (*diyah*—blood money—will be paid to the victim's family, or women from the offender's family will be married to men from the victim's family. The children will always join their father's side). After all, warriors are in great demand, and blood feuds within the extended family could leave it vulnerable to its rivals. Thus, although not unheard of, it is quite rare for relatives within the khams to spill one another's blood. Moreover, this author is unaware of a single case when, in response to an offense performed by members of a khams against an important member or a shaykh, in this case Saddam Husayn, the whole five-generation family unit has banded together to kill the offenders. Saddam's decision to call on his khams to kill the defectors was, to say the least, unprecedented.

Saddam perverted the tribal code in other ways. Kamil Hassan, the defectors' father, was innocent because he never left Iraq, and so the blood feud should not have extended to him. Once the offenders themselves had been punished, there was no need to punish any other male members of the family. Moreover, according to tribal custom, women are *never* involved in blood revenge, yet Husayn Kamil's sisters and other female members of his immediate family were also victims of the carnage.

Although the elimination of the Kamils probably did not create any immediate threat to Saddam's personal safety or his rule, it does pose a longer-term danger to the cohesiveness of his family. Saddam had promised the defectors amnesty, and immediately after the attack he claimed that he had not been involved. He explicitly endorsed the killings—which "purified" the family by amputating from the "hand" an "ailing finger"— but he also assured Iraqis that had he been notified about it ahead of time he would have prevented the assault because, "when I pardon, I mean it."[31] By making sure that so many members of the family were involved in the murders, Saddam deflected guilt from himself and so made it extremely difficult for an embittered extended family member to single him out as the target of a retributory blood feud. At the very least, all those with the Kamils' blood on their hands will rally to the president in such a situation. Of course, even had he not ordered the killings, according to the tribal code, as a member of the khams (indeed, the most important person in it) he still bears responsibility for its decisions, so it is not unthinkable that Saddam might be targeted by a vendetta. Of course, the tremendous security around Saddam makes it very unlikely that even a family member could actually assassinate him. Consequently, if they are out for revenge, members likely will opt to hit an easier target than the president. Already there are unconfirmed reports suggesting that those family members who did not participate in the attack are demanding the murderers pay huge sums of money as diyah.[32] If true, and if these debts remain unsettled, there may be individual cases of blood-letting within the extended family. Almost certainly, accounts will be settled after Saddam disappears from the scene.

As a final thought, a lingering question with important clues regarding the cohesiveness of Saddam's family is, Why did the Kamils opt to return to Iraq after they defected to Jordan? Saddam's record of keeping promises is a checkered one at best, and no one is more aware of this than his closest lieutenants and his family. We now know that Husayn Kamil's decision to defect was precipitated by 'Udayy's threat to put him on trial for corruption or to assassinate him. Yet, with the wisdom of hindsight, this decision was almost certainly an overreaction. 'Udayy's ability actually to prosecute Husayn Kamil was probably slight because Saddam remained firmly behind his son-in-law. Also, Husayn Kamil was protected by bodyguards, and his brother was co-commander of *al-Amn al-Khass*, the Special Security Organization (SSO). Assassinating him then would not have been an easy task, even for 'Udayy. Although we may never know what ultimately prompted his decision to return, Kamil seems to have overreacted again, this time to the disappointment he found in Amman. Once the dust of his sensational defection had settled, few Iraqis rallied to his banner, and neither Jordan nor the United States showed much enthusiasm for him as a potential leader of the Iraqi opposition and eventual replacement for Saddam. Despite his public disclosures of Iraq's malfeasance and his implied calls for Saddam's overthrow, Husayn Kamil never denounced Saddam explicitly. He must have calculated that this, and his powerful family, could ensure that the president would keep his word if he returned. But the proclamation of the tashmis/ hadar al-dam ought to have been a clear sign that he had lost his family's support. This warning was not lost on the rest of his family—his brothers and cousins desperately objected to his decision to go back. Indeed, Husayn Kamil's course was so obviously foolish—and so out of character for a man universally regarded as "a cold fish," in the words of one Iraqi expatriate— that it raises the possibility that the brain tumor and major surgery he underwent in Amman in February 1994 may have impaired his judgment or otherwise affected his personality.[33]

THE ATTEMPTED ASSASSINATION OF 'UDAYY

At 7 p.m. on December 12, 1996, in Hayy al-Mutanabbi in west Baghdad's al-Mansur quarter, 'Udayy Saddam Husayn was shot by a group of four or five people and badly wounded. He was treated by French neurosurgeons in Baghdad but was refused an entry visa for medical care in France. According to French reports, even after long hours in the operating room, four bullets remained lodged in his spine and pelvis, and he was paralyzed from the waist down.[34] A few months later, Udayy was operated on again; this time they were able to remove the remaining bullets, and since then he has begun a slow recovery.

That someone wanted to kill 'Udayy Saddam Husayn is hardly surprising given his notoriety; that they were able to nearly do so is fairly remarkable. At least six opposition organizations claimed responsibility for the attack.[35] Yet, it is highly unlikely that an opposition group by itself could have penetrated the heavy security and secrecy surrounding the movements of all members of the president's family. Consequently, it is much more likely that the attempt on 'Udayy was at least in part an inside job. Unfortunately, we have only bits and pieces of evidence to speculate about the would-be assassins. The attack might have been performed by relatives of the Kamils. Two of Saddam's cousins were buried in a state funeral after the murder of the Kamils and were hailed as martyrs for participating in the attack, but there is some reason to believe that they may actually have been killed *defending* the Kamils. Rumors to this effect were widespread in Baghdad at the time.[36] Alternatively, Watban and Sib'awi Ibrahim certainly had cause to want their nephew dead. Although Watban and Sib'awi almost certainly were not personally involved in the attack (their generation has always been very loyal to the extended family), younger members of their side of the family may have taken it upon themselves to avenge their older relatives' honor. According to one source, Saddam felt the need to interrogate both Watban and Sib'awi, as well as their nephew Namir, son of their deceased brother Dahham.[37]

It appears most likely, however, that members of the al-Haza' extended family were responsible for the assassination attempt. The al-Haza' is one of fourteen *buyutat* (houses or households) of 'Umar III, an important *fakhdh* (subtribal unit) within Saddam's al-Bu Nasir tribe. According to various sources, the leader of the cabal was Ra'd, an army officer and a nephew of Gen. 'Umar Muhammad al-Haza', the former shaykh of the "house." In 1986, General al-Haza' was tortured and executed by Saddam for bad-mouthing him after Iraq's defeat in the first Battle of al-Faw during the war with Iran. According to numerous sources, the al-Haza' never forgot this, and Ra'd sought to avenge their shaykh's death by killing 'Udayy. These same sources claim that although Ra'd was the moving force in the attack, the actual shooting was done by an opposition group called al-Nahda. Ra'd provided them with the information, they performed the hit, and according to some sources they all escaped to western Iraq, after which the

Dulaym tribe helped them escape to Jordan and from there to the West. According to others, however, they fled to Iran.[38] The Iraq National Congress (INC) reports that soon after the initial attack, other members of al-Nahda tried to finish the job and kill 'Udayy in the hospital, but they were themselves killed by the SSO guards protecting 'Udayy.

The attack on 'Udayy was a major blow to the regime because it revealed a chink in the armor of Saddam's security apparatus—including the *al-Himaya* (Palace Guard) who failed to protect Saddam's favorite child, and the *mukhabarat,* the all-powerful intelligence service—which allowed the assassins to escape unharmed. In typical fashion, the regime moved quickly to restore the reputation of its security services and deflect rumors of an inside job that suggested opposition to Saddam within the ruling circle. Iraqi security arrested several hundred people. Some of those arrested were members of various internal security organs, reflecting the regime's own suspicion that the attack was an inside job. Others arrested were people who lived in the neighborhood where the attempt took place.[39] Meanwhile, Baghdad's propaganda organs claimed, as they had on other occasions in the past, that foreign powers conducted the attack to try to undermine Iraq's stability. This time they blamed Iran. 'Udayy, from his hospital wheelchair, testified in a TV interview that his attackers "did not look Arab! They looked different! . . . In the past we have found out that Iran is [usually] involved in such incidents."[40] To give weight to its claims, Iraq demanded that Iran extradite the *Da'wa*—oppositionists who were responsible for several attacks on regime figures since the early 1980s and who later fled to Iran—and even lodged formal requests with the UN Security Council to this effect. Iran flatly denied any connection to the whole affair.[41] Nevertheless, the Iraqis ordered their pet Iranian opposition fighters, the National Resistance Council of Iran, or *Mujahidin e-Khalq* (MEK), to "retaliate" with terrorist acts in Iran. In response, Iranian agents launched a mortar attack against the MEK's office in downtown Baghdad, apparently injuring dozens of Iraqi citizens.[42]

Until 'Udayy is convinced that the authorities have managed to arrest all of his assailants, he is likely to continue to seek revenge. This may further erode the family's cohesion as 'Udayy searches for accomplices within the family and pursues members of other powerful tribes who have influence within the al-Bu Nasir and the president's family. Thus, 'Udayy is likely to be a thorn in his father's side as soon as he gets better. He was violent and unpredictable before he was crippled, and now, having partially lost the use of his legs, he is probably a bitter and deeply frustrated man. This makes him something of a human time bomb that could explode at any time and on anyone. In particular, if he is again put in charge of the Fida'iyyin Saddam or some other institution with military capabilities, he is very likely to use them against his real and perceived enemies both inside the family and out.

Indeed, the extended family is probably Saddam's greatest source of problems at the moment. According to widespread rumors, Saddam placed his wife, Sajida, under house arrest in his palace near Tikrit in response to a lengthy fight they had related to some aspect of 'Udayy's injury.[43] To refute the story, Saddam briefly paraded her in front of the TV cameras, but this merely convinced skeptical Iraqis that she was still alive. Sajida's alleged involvement may be explained by her closeness with 'Udayy. In addition to any special affection she may have for her eldest son, ever since 'Udayy murdered Hanna Jojo, Saddam's bodyguard and food-taster, on October 18, 1988, Sajida has always taken his side against his father in their frequent quarrels. ('Udayy killed Hanna Jojo because of the latter's disobedience and because he was believed to be procuring mistresses for Saddam, which 'Udayy considered an affront to his mother's honor.) When Saddam arrested 'Udayy for the murder—conducted in public at a state dinner—Sajida interceded, objecting to the arrest and to Saddam's decision to try him. In the end she triumphed, as 'Udayy was pardoned before he was even put on trial. Nevertheless, the affair created the first major crisis between Saddam and his wife, and Sajida spent several months abroad. Although she later returned to Iraq and Saddam has gone to great lengths to paint himself as a loving and revered husband and father, their relations never fully recovered.

FRICTIONS WITHIN THE AL-BU NASIR

Beyond his extended family, frictions have also developed within Saddam's al-Bu Nasir tribe.[44] The flare-up of problems with the al-Haza' household in connection with the attack on 'Udayy is only one of these problems.[45] According to some reports, another of al-Bu Nasir's households, Aal Nada (or Aal Husayn), has also become estranged from the president. The Aal Nada are the offspring of Nada ibn Husayn Bek, who are paternal cousins seven generations removed from Saddam.[46] Periodic reporting has made clear that they have been at odds with the president since early 1996, although the reasons for this are not clear. Rumors in Iraq have suggested that they refused to participate in the assassination of the Kamils in February 1996; however, this claim appears unfounded.[47] Being eight generations removed from Saddam and his male children—counting always starts with the youngest males—the Aal Nada do not belong to Saddam's khams and therefore did not have a stake in that feud. If the Aal Nada had participated, this would have muddied the strong signal Saddam was trying to send that this was an issue decided by the khams according to tribal traditions.

These new divisions within the tribe have added to longer-standing problems Saddam has with several other al-Bu Nasir households. The Aal Bakr have been estranged from Saddam for more than fifteen years. This is the household of Saddam's predecessor as president, Gen. Ahmad Hasan al-Bakr, whom Saddam is widely believed to have ordered poisoned in 1982. In addition to this source of tension, Bakr's widow is a member of the Aal Nada family, creating an additional link between these two disgruntled branches of the tribe. The al-Masallat, too, are at least partly estranged. This household includes the president's wife, Sajida, as well as his half-brothers the Ibrahims, and Sajida's brother, the late Gen. 'Adnan Khayr Allah Talfah—widely, and apparently incorrectly, believed to have been killed by Saddam in a helicopter crash.[48] Saddam also sacked all three of the Ibrahim brothers from their lofty posts and, not having punished his son, must bear responsibility for 'Udayy's shooting of Watban Ibrahim. All three "houses" belong to the pretigious 'Umar Beg III subtribal unit. Yet another discontented household (albeit more distant from Saddam's al-Majid branch than the Aal Bakr, Aal Masallat, and Aal Nada) is the al-Bu Musa Faraj, who continue to chafe over the unexplained execution of one of their most illustrious sons, Maj. Gen. Dr. Fadil al-Barrak, former chief of General Intelligence, in the early 1990s.

These schisms within Saddam's tribe are a problem for the president, but they are not crippling in and of themselves. The al-Bu Nasir is a medium-sized tribe, numbering some 25,000 people. It has many houses and first came into existence fourteen generations before Saddam. Thus the enmity of even five or six houses should not be misconstrued as a sign that the president's tribe is slowly turning against him: There are many other houses that remain loyal, receive tremendous benefits from their association with the president, and would fight any challengers to his rule. At the same time, disgruntled households cannot be dismissed, especially since several of those currently estranged from Saddam are quite powerful. The al-Haza', Aal Bakr, Aal Nada, and Aal Masallat are all part of the 'Umar

al-Bu Nasir: Saddam Husayn's Tribe

The *buyutat* (houses), or *afkhadh* (subtribal units) with an asterisk are those at least partially estranged from Saddam, because of various controversies; the names in **bold sans serif** type are members of Saddam's *khams*, or five-generation family unit. Each column represents a different generation, but not necessarily a corresponding time period; sons are not necessarily listed by age.

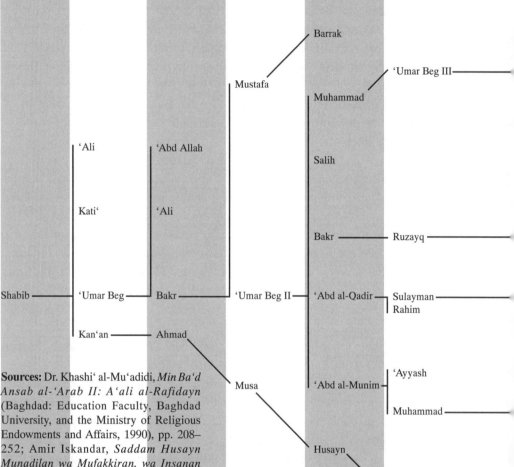

Sources: Dr. Khashi' al-Mu'adidi, *Min Ba'd Ansab al-'Arab II: A'ali al-Rafidayn* (Baghdad: Education Faculty, Baghdad University, and the Ministry of Religious Endowments and Affairs, 1990), pp. 208–252; Amir Iskandar, *Saddam Husayn Munadilan wa Mufakkiran, wa Insanan* (Paris: Hachette, 1980), p. 21; Yunis al-Shaykh Ibrahim al-Samarra'i, *Qaba'il al-'Iraq* (Baghdad: al-Sharq al-Jadid, 1989), pp. 655–658; Yunis al-Shaykh Ibrahim Samarra'i, *Al-Qaba'il Wal Buyutat al-Hashimiyya fi al-'Iraq* (Baghdad: al-Sharq al-Jadid, 1988), pp. 30–32; and the author's personal interviews. Reprinted with permission of the U.S. Institute of Peace.

[1] Note: Saddam's son-in-law, Husayn Kamil, had a son who was not amongst those killed after Husayn Kamil returned to Iraq. His brother Saddam had three sons who also survived him. For purposes of space, 'Ali Husayn Kamil and his cousins are not listed as a separate generation on this family tree.

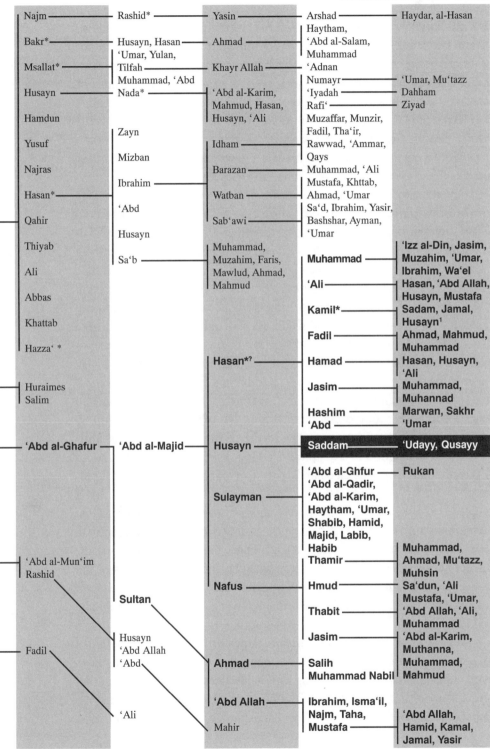

Bek al-Thalith subtribal unit (*fakhdh*), the largest in al-Bu Nasir.[49] Having several key houses of this subunit oppose him creates the risk that, at some point, the entire 'Umar Bek al-Thalith may turn against him or, because of their influence within the larger tribe, even all of al-Bu Nasir. At present, this threat seems remote. For instance, 'Abd al-Hamid Mahmud (or Humud), the shaykh of both al-Bu Nasir and Aal Khattab—the leading house within 'Umar Bek al-Thalith—firmly supports Saddam and currently serves as his Chief Companion. The same may be said about Arshad Yasin Rashid, another Chief Companion from 'Umar al-Thalith.

Nevertheless, it is clear that, within his tribe, too, Saddam is facing growing difficulties that are likely to influence his behavior. When he considers sensitive security appointments he can no longer trust all of his fellow tribesmen equally. He is likely to place less authority in the hands of members of some households (and potentially some larger subunits) than others. At present Saddam is the only person who can keep the tribe in power, and losing its privileged position is a concern great enough to keep the al-Bu Nasir united behind him. But increasingly, Saddam cannot take this solidarity for granted. For Saddam, his tribe is not only his strongest base of support but also the greatest potential threat to his rule. The al-Bu Nasir is the only tribe that still has large numbers of representatives in all important state security organs and is therefore the tribe best positioned to stage a successful coup d'état against him. No other tribe can claim so many of its members in so many key positions throughout the Iraqi military and government. For example, Maj. Gen. Kamal Mustafa 'Abd Allah is the commander of the Special Republican Guard, Maj. Gen. Tariq al-Haza' al-Nasiri is a provincial governor; Lt. Gen. Nasir Sa'id Tawfiq 'Abd al-Ghafur al-Nasiri commands one of Iraq's five army corps; and Brig Gen. Kamil Mustafa 'Abd Allah al-Nasiri commands one of the six Republican Guard divisions. Indeed, the Republican Guard, the army, and Iraq's intelligence services team have many men with the common surnames of the al-Bu Nasir, in addition to al-Nasiri—surnames such as Khattab, Haza', Najam, Qahir, 'Abbas, 'Abd al-Qadir (or Qadir), 'Abd al-Ghafur, Nada, and Faraj.

At present, al-Bu Nasir still pins its hopes on Saddam. He continues to demonstrate his skill in keeping the country firmly in hand and shows every sign of eventually wriggling out of the international embargo that binds Iraq so tightly. Saddam has gone to great lengths to cushion the impact of the sanctions on his fellow tribesmen to ensure their continued loyalty. Moreover, any move against Saddam poses an unacceptable risk to the position of the tribe—even if the coup were successful and were conducted by other members of the tribe, it could ignite a period of chaos in which the al-Bu Nasir could be deposed by another of the main Sunni tribes; and, if Iraqi society goes through much deeper changes, the fate of the whole ruling elite may be in jeopardy. Thus, for al-Bu Nasir, Saddam's continued rule remains a far more attractive alternative to the risks inherent in trying to replace him. On the other hand, if the members of al-Bu Nasir begin to feel the economic pinch of the embargo or conclude that an Iraq led by Saddam is guaranteed a future of eternal poverty and military defeats, losses, and inferiority—even if the tribe itself is provided for—some may change their minds. Indeed, the fear that the deepening impact of sanctions was finally beginning to affect his own tribesmen seems to have been an important factor in Saddam's decision to accept UN Security Council Resolution 986. Saddam apparently conceded that without some increase in the flow of food and other supplies into Iraq, he would not be able to assure this key element of his power base that he could provide for them.

SADDAM'S PAN-TRIBAL COALITION: SOURCE OF STRENGTH OR THREAT?

Since it took power in July 1968, the Ba'th party has had a love-hate relationship with Iraq's tribes. Ba'thist ideology committed the party to the elimination of all traces of "tribalism" and "feudalism." Yet, in practice it has cultivated many tribal shaykhs and used them as mediators between the regime and those areas of rural Iraq still dominated by tribes. Moreover, during the Iran–Iraq War, the tribes became an important element of Saddam's power base. At that time, he began the large-scale recruitment of young tribesmen into his internal security and key military units. As he saw it, the tribesmen were uncorrupted by city life and retained the desert codes of honor. To them, surrendering in battle was unthinkable. Also, Saddam saw in the tribes pure Arabs who would always remain loyal to the the Arab regime in Baghdad and would fiercely oppose Iranian expansion. This recruitment policy was aimed mainly (though not exclusively) at Sunni Arab tribes. In addition to Saddam's own al-Bu Nasir, preference was given to a number of tribes and tribal federations that traditionally had good relations with al-Bu Nasir.

Thus, Saddam and the Ba'th formed a loose confederation of tribes and (less so) nontribal village populations that acted as the principal pillars of the regime and furnished it with a pool of loyal manpower available for sensitive postings. At least during the first two decades of Ba'thist rule, the nontribal population of Saddam's hometown of Tikrit worked with members of the al-Bu Nasir—also called al-Beigat—some of whom resided in a separate quarter of the town. As for the prominent tribes connected with the al-Bu Nasir, one of the most important was the Jubbur, which hailed primarily from the Tikrit area but also from other governorates, mainly around Mosul. Yet, Jubbur tribesmen immediately south of Baghdad were not included as much in this select group because they were too powerful and too close to the capital city for comfort. Other tribes traditionally close to al-Bu Nasir included the 'Ubayd, most of whose members lived immediately north of Baghdad; the large Dulaym federation to the west of Baghdad; and the large Shammar Jarbah federation in the Jazirah, west and northwest of Baghdad. In addition to these large tribal federations, Saddam's tribal coalition also included a number of lesser, albeit still important, tribes; among them:

- the Harb from the area of Dur, and nontribal Duris and people from the vicinity of Dur;

- the 'Aqaydat, from southwest of Mosul;

- the Khazraj, from west of the Tigris between Baghdad and Samarra (and some in Mosul);

- al-Mushahada, from south of the Khazraj;

- al-'Azza, from between the Tigris and the Iranian border north of Baghdad; and

- the old and powerful Sa'dun clan from the deep south around Nasiriyya.

Other than the Jubbur, a mixed tribe with a sizable Shi'i complement south of al-Hillah and the Shammar, which has a large branch in the Shi'i South (Shammar Toqa), all of these tribes were entirely, or nearly entirely, Sunni Arab tribes. Yet, several Shi'i tribes from southern Iraq also became firm supporters of Saddam and his regime. In particular, the Banu Hasan (or Hisan) had cast its lot with the regime almost immediately after it came to power in 1968. Al-Bu Nasir itself also has a Shi'i branch in the South. Many other Shi'i tribes accepted Ba'th rule and became passive supporters for lack of any other option.

The core tribes as collective entities gained in prestige and power from their association with the regime, and those of their members recruited into the military and the security services found an honorable way of making a living. Many joined the Republican Guard, the Himaya, and the *al-Amn al-Khass* (the Special Security Organization, the first ring around the President's Palace), and those who joined the regular army were promoted more rapidly than their nontribal colleagues.

By and large, the relationship was also beneficial to the regime, assuring them of a preexisting power structure they could easily tap into to control the countryside and large numbers of men they could more readily trust to guard the interests of the regime against all challengers. Yet, in recent years, Saddam has found that this situation cuts both ways. The presence of so many tribesmen within the elite military units and security services also gave them the access to Saddam and the levers of power needed to overthrow the regime, while their tribal loyalties occasionally took precedence over their loyalty to the regime and furnished a ready-made network to recruit coup plotters. Saddam exposed the first tribally organized plot in January 1990, when he preempted a Jubbur-led coup d'état. After he executed scores of Jubburi army and Republican Guard officers, he reassigned the (many) remaining Jubburi officers, making sure that they would never again be in a position to hatch a military coup on their own.[50] Following unexplained tensions with the 'Ubayd in 1993, that tribe's officers, too, were reassigned. The torture and execution of Air Force Maj. Gen. Muhammad Mazlum al-Dulaymi provoked a local revolt of al-Bu Nimr of the Dulaym federation in and around Ramadi, west of Baghdad, on May 17, 1995. This revolt did not even encompass the whole of al-Bu Nimr, let alone the entire Dulaym tribal federation, and it was crushed in two or three weeks. Nevertheless, it introduced a new element of mistrust into the relationship between Saddam and yet another of the large Sunni Arab tribal groups. There are still many Dulaymis in key posts throughout the various military and intelligence services, but the regime must feel somewhat more uneasy about their presence.[51]

Thus, Saddam Husayn's relations with at least three major Sunni tribal groups—the Jubbur, the Dulaym, and the 'Ubayd—are ailing. His high-profile visit to the Dulaym precisely one Islamic (*Hijri*) year after their revolt made clear the extent of his concern about this situation. Saddam must have found this visit somewhat reassuring, as the tribal shaykhs and 'ulama assured him of the total loyalty of the sons of Anbar (that is, the Dulaym) and their readiness to sacrifice themselves for president and country. Saddam then addressed the tribal leaders and gave a lengthy speech in which he alluded both to the Dulaymi rebels as well as to Gen. Husayn Kamil, and argued that treason was incited not by the party's message, but in the weakness of the traitors in the face of hardship. Not all those who started the march of the Ba'th Revolution, he noted, would necessarily complete it. No one is immune to weakness, Saddam warned, and even blood relations may become traitors, as happened with a member of the president's own family who "betrayed us . . . hurt his family . . . very badly." The president further explained that the family had to cleanse itself by killing the traitors; otherwise everybody "would have been entitled to stone them." Finally, Saddam praised the Dulaym. By coming to meet him (not that they had a choice), he said they proved that they had dissociated themselves from those who "did wrong . . . bad and weak people . . . who deviated from the true path." But he also implied that they had to do more: Like his own family, it was their duty to kill any member of the tribe who deviated.[52] In so doing, Saddam endeavored to reshape tribal norms to suit his own security needs: hadar al-dam and tashmis were no longer sufficient. Like the president's family, the tribes, too, were now expected to kill their "renegades" with their own hands. If not, they themselves would be susceptible to being "stoned."

The president's effort to restore the position of the Dulaym demonstrated his desire to continue to rely on the tribes in their long-standing roles as pillars of his regime and sources of loyal manpower. Indeed, Saddam has generally tolerated the presence of even large numbers of Jubburis in the Republican Guard and internal security organs. For example, Jubburis reportedly still constitute up to 50 percent of the Republican Guard, while Dulaymis make up roughly one-third of the total.[53] Even if these figures are inflated, as they seem to be, they provide a general indication of the centrality of the two tribes (or tribal federations) to the regime.

Saddam's willingness to allow men from these tribes to continue to serve in the armed forces and security services, often still in highly sensitive senior positions, may be explained in two ways. First, as a tribal peasant himself he is aware that, in the words of Dale Eickelman, tribal affinities "provided a range of potential identities . . . [rather than] a base for sustained collective action."[54] In other words, tribal ties are essentially practical links *reflecting* existing ties, rather than formal lineage classifications that *dictated* political action. The federations are decentralized and every tribe is left very much to itself. Even within the individual member-tribes there is little unity of purpose and each subtribal unit (*fakhdh*) usually has its own priorities. As a glaring example of these sorts of problems, the Dulaym uprising of May 17, 1995, spread to only a part of al-Bu Nimr. The revolt exposed the inherent difficulty of a massive tribal revolt: More often than not, tribal officers and officials give priority to the interests of their extended, or even nuclear, families over those of the *fakhdh,* the *al-'ashira* (tribe), or the *al-qabila* (tribal federation). Second, the size of Saddam's elite military and intelligence organizations require large numbers of trustworthy officials. Therefore, Saddam has to trust someone to occupy these posts, and he apparently has concluded that the instances of disloyalty in these large Sunni tribes do not necessarily call into question the loyalty of all of their members. He still believes that the Sunni tribesmen are generally more loyal to him than Iraq's nontribal population and thus when forced to put someone in a position of authority, he still tends to favor members of the Sunni tribes that have traditionally been his most loyal supporters.

Nevertheless, Saddam Husayn has not survived as undisputed ruler of Iraq for nineteen years by taking risks. He has taken numerous precautions to neutralize any remaining threats from those tribes whose members have already shown themselves to merit suspicion. According to a former senior officer in the Guard, after the Gulf War, Saddam transferred large number of officers hailing from the Jubbur and Dulaym out of the Special Republican Guard (the inner circle within the Republican Guard, which provides the garrison of the city of Baghdad, guards Saddam's palaces and key government buildings, and is responsible for hiding Iraq's proscribed weapons of mass destruction arsenal). Instead, Saddam replaced them with officers originating from smaller and weaker tribes.[55] So far, this policy seems to have worked well. Since 1991, several military coups d'état have been discovered and exposed before they could gather any real momentum. Of greatest importance, in all of the most recent cases, there was no common tribal foundation to the cabals. This means that a successful coup will require military personnel from a number of tribes to cooperate, and it may have to reach out to nontribal officers as well. The bonds of tribal loyalty had been a powerful guarantee of secrecy for would-be assassins in the past, and the difficulty of organizing tribally based coup attempts now substantially increases the risk of a leak.[56] In other words, Saddam has managed to benefit from Iraq's tribal system without paying an unacceptable security price: He can count on the loyalty of his own tribe (for the most part) and several others as buttresses to his regime, but disloyal officers cannot use their tribal networks to organize an effective plot against him.

The regime also appears to have the tribes well under control even in their own lands. It should be noted that Saddam generally has not experienced many problems with tribal revolts (as opposed to tribally based coup plots). With the exception of guerrilla activities in the southern marshes, which are supported by some of the Shi'i tribes, only a small number of Shi'i tribes have revolted since the Shi'i *intifada* (uprising) of March 1991.[57] Indeed, even during the intifada, many Shi'i tribes took no part in the revolt, and a few—such as the Khaffaja from near Nasiriyya, the Aal Ribbat, and the Bani Hasan (or Hisan) from the Kufa area—even supported the regime.

Overall, the threat of a large-scale tribal uprising currently appears remote. The intifada was primarily a city phenomenon, and those tribes that did revolt were punished severely.[58] In addition, the larger Shi'i tribes have generally been broken down into smaller units than their Sunni counterparts, as a result of both deliberate Ottoman efforts beginning in the late 1860s to break the cohesiveness of the Shi'i tribes and natural causes like changes in the course of the Euphrates river, which forced parts of some tribes to leave their traditional lands and caused others to compete for land, water, and other resources. On the other hand, the Sunni tribes have so far largely remained loyal to the regime. Were they to decide to confront Saddam, they would face serious difficulties. The regime has systematically broken up those tribes close to the capital (like the Jubbur south of Baghdad) into smaller units by settling other tribes in their midst. Of course, there are still several very large tribal federations in Iraq, but they are relatively distant from Baghdad. Moreover, even the largest tribes are virtually powerless against the forces that the state can wield. The Dulaym, along the Euphrates west of the capital, and the Shammar, in the Jazirah, are huge federations consisting of hundreds of thousands of people each. Similarly, the Jubbur north and north west of the capital are a large tribe. The Mushahida, al-Bu 'Amir, Banu Tamim, Khazraj, and 'Azza—all immediately north of Baghdad—are smaller but more closely knit and closer to the capital. All of these tribes have rifles; some also have mortars and heavy machine guns. But they are extremely short of ammunition and none of their weapons are a match for the tanks of the Republican Guard or the helicopter gunships of the regular army. No less important, the tribes lack a central authority that would allow them to coordinate their actions against the regime effectively. Finally, many in the Sunni Arab population of Iraq are concerned about the possibility of a new Shi'i revolt, certainly if it is supported by Iran. Saddam's propaganda machine enhanced such fears after the 1991 intifada in the South. By executing Sunni party officials who had surrendered, the Shi'i rebels did not make things easier. This concern helps Saddam win much Sunni Arab support.

NOTES

1   An interview with a senior official with the United Nations Special Commission on Iraq (UNSCOM), New York, October 13, 1995.

2   For example, see *al-Jumhuriyya,* September 21, 1991, in the *Foreign Broadcast Information Service–Near East and South Asia–Daily Report (FBIS-NES-DR),* September 26, 1991, pp. 21–23.

3   A speech to tribal chiefs in al-Anbar, *Iraqi News Agency (INA),* May 7, 1996.

4   See *INA,* August 17, 1995, in *FBIS-NES-DR,* August 18, 1995, p. 20. The public was warned that any financial or commercial relations with Kamil Hasan al-Majid had to be reported to the authorities.

5   In Palestinian and Sinai Arab–Bedouin vernacular, it is called *tashmis* (exposing to the scorching sun). 'Ali Hasan al-Majid, Husayn Kamil's paternal uncle, interviewed on *Iraqi TV,* August 12, 1995, in *FBIS-NES-DR,* August 14, 1995, pp. 37–38. *Hadar al-dam* of enemies of the regime, if they belonged to one's own tribe, was a common part of tribal shaykhs' swearing of allegiance to Saddam; see for example *al-'Iraq,* December 1, 1992. For *tashmis,* see Joseph Ginat, *Blood Revenge* (Brighton: Sussex Academic Press, 1997), pp. 100ff.

6   *SAIRI Radio,* September 2, 1997, in *BBC Summary of World Broadcasts,* September 4, 1997.

7   Sultan's great grandfather was the brother of Saddam's grandfather 'Abd al-Majid. For Saddam's family tree see Amir Iskandar, *Saddam Husayn, Munadilan wa Mufakkiran wa Insanan* (Saddam Husayn as a Struggler, a Thinker, and a Man) (Paris: Hachette, 1980), p. 21; for more see Ibrahim al-Shaykh al-Samarra'i, *al-Qaba'il al-'Iraqiyya (The Iraqi Tribes)* (Baghdad: al-Sharq al-Jadid, 1989), pp. 655–658. For the family tree, see pp. 22–23 herein.

8   Based on an interview with a person who accidentally saw some remnants of the incinerated cars a few years later. The burned garage has been standing, untouched, since 1995—a monument to 'Udayy's folly.

9   See *Jordan Times,* October 5–6, 1995.

10 See *al-Ra'y*, August 16, 1996, quoting a *Babil* attack on the Ministry of Culture and Information for closing it down for four days. The daily did not actually receive official permission to publish until May 1992.

11 'Udayy attended at least one regular cabinet meeting to present his proposals "to develop the youth sector"; see *Republic of Iraq Radio Network*, December 12, 1993, in *FBIS-NES-DR*, December 14, 1993, p. 38.

12 See *al-'Iraq*, November 29, 1995. The new chairman was a party functionary.

13 See the report in the usually well-informed *al-Sharq al-Awsat*, March 21, 1996.

14 At the spectacular state ceremonies, 'Udayy boasted of two feathers in his cap: command of the Fida'iyyin and the "Lion Cubs" (children, 9–15 years old, trained to become Fida'iyyin), and the weapons-repairs operation; see *al-Thawra*, April 30, 1995, in *FBIS-NES-DR*, June 6, 1996, pp. 32–34. See also a report of an air show demonstrating aircraft "repaired" by 'Udayy's technical teams: *al-Thawra*, August 3, 1995, in *FBIS-NES-DR*, August 23, 1995, pp. 36–37. These sources also provide information on both organizations.

15 See *al-Thawra* (Baghdad), July 21, 1996, for an interview with the general on the Fida'iyyin and the Cubs, in *FBIS-NES-DR*, July 29, 1996, pp. 31–32. Already in March it leaked out that 'Udayy lost the command. See *al-Sharq al-Awsat*, March 21, 1996.

16 See *al-Sharq al-Awsat*, November 16, 1995, in *FBIS-NES-DR*, November 17, 1995, p. 17. This report is confirmed by interviews with British and American officials in London and Washington, October 1995. Since 1997, 'Udayy has started a slow and arduous comeback. He was again "elected" president of the General Union of Iraqi Youth as well as the chairman of its executive committee. But despite 'Udayy's pleading, Saddam has deferred 'Udayy's return to command of the Fida'iyyin until some unforeseen day "when the call of jihad is made," whatever that may mean. See *INA*, November 4, 1997, in *FBIS-NES-DR*, November 4, 1997. For the report on the Union of Iraqi Youth, see *al-Jumhuriyya*, September 24, 1997, in *FBIS-NES-DR*, September 29, 1997.

17 See *Yedi'ot Aharonot*, August 14, 1995.

18 See *Agence France Presse (AFP)*, August 10 1995, in *FBIS-NES-DR*, August 10, 1995, p. 38.

19 See *al-Sharq al-Awsat* quoting Iraqi embassy sources from Amman, February 15 and 25, 1994.

20 See *al-Thawra*, April 30, 1995, in *FBIS-NES-DR*, June 6, 1996, pp. 32–34.

21 Based on interviews with Western officials. For slightly different versions see *al-Bilad,* August 16, 1995, in *FBIS-NES-DR,* August 17, 1995, pp. 27–28; *London Iraqi Broadcasting Corp. Press Release,* August 16, 1995, in *FBIS-NES-DR,* August 17, 1995, pp. 30–31; and *al-Sharq al-Awsat,* August 17 and 18, 1995, in *FBIS-NES-DR,* August 18, 1995, pp. 20–21, 37. The defection was the combined result of 'Udayy's bodyguards' assault on Watban and Kamil's fear that the president was turning against him. In his meeting with the king and 'Udayy, Kamil accused 'Udayy of threatening to eliminate him.

22 *Reuters,* August 31, 1995.

23 See *Iraqi TV,* August 20, 1995, in *FBIS-NES-DR,* August 21, 1995, p. 36; *New York Times,* August 18, 1995.

24 Interviews with Western officials. See also *al-Sharq al-Awsat,* November 16, 1995, in *FBIS-NES-DR,* November 17, 1995, p. 17.

25 See *al-Sharq al-Awsat,* November 16, 1995, in *FBIS-NES-DR,* November 17, 1995, p. 17; this account has been confirmed by interviews with Western officials.

26 See Saddam Husayn, speech to tribal chiefs in al-Anbar, *INA* newswire, May 7, 1996.

27 See Saddam's family tree herein, pp. 22–23.

28 See *al-Jumhuriyya,* February 24, 1996.

29 See, for example, *al-Mu'tamar* (published in London by the Iraq National Congress), November 22, 1996, p. 2.

30 See *al-Jumhuriyya,* February 24, 1996. In Iraqi tribal society, the five generations of a khams are counted from the youngest males in the family backward. Thus, because Saddam's sons, Udayy and Qusayy had no male children in February 1996, they were the first generation in Saddam's khams.

31 See *INA,* February 23–24, 1996, in *FBIS-NES-DR,* February 26, 1996, p. 19. For information on the sisters' death, see *AFP,* February 26, 1996, in *FBIS-NES-DR,* February 27, 1966, pp. 23–24. See also *al-Majalla,* March 17–23, 1996, in *FBIS-NES-DR,* March 22, 1996, pp. 19–20. For an article claiming that Saddam endorsed the murders, see *Associated Press* quoting *INA,* May 10, 1996. Gen. Nizar al-Khazraji, who defected after the murder, however, did not mention the sisters and their families among the casualties; see his interview in *al-Hayat,* April 16, 1996.

32 See for example, *al-Aswaq,* January 22, 1997, quoting new arrivals from Baghdad. According to this report, since early December 1996 Husayn Kamil has been partially rehabilitated secretly, dubbed "Martyr of the Tribal Wrath."

If true, this is an indication that the murder is still a stormy issue.

33 See, for example, *al-Sharq al-Awsat,* February 15, 1994.

34 See *AFP,* January 20, 1997, in *FBIS-Serial NC2001125597,* January 20, 1997. See also an interview with Gen. Binford Peay, commander of the U.S. Central Command, *Los Angeles Times,* January 10, 1997; and *Paris Radio Monte Carlo,* December 13, 1996, in *FBIS-Serial JN312125396,* December 13, 1996.

35 See the publication of *Qadaya 'Iraqiyya* (the Iraq Foundation), a Washington-based nongovernmental organization, December 1996, p. 18.

36 See Walid Abu Zahr, *al-Watan al-'Arabi,* December 27, 1996, in *FBIS-Serial JN3012205596,* December 27, 1996.

37 Huda Husseini, *al-Sharq al-Awsat,* December 14, 1996, in *FBIS-Serial MM1612111896,* December 16, 1996.

38 Based on an interview with a well-informed source, London, July 11, 1997. See, for example, Kamaran Karadaghi, *al-Hayat,* January 24, 1997, as quoted in *Mideast Mirror,* January 24, 1997. For a somewhat different version see Patrick Cockburn, *Independent*, January 23, 1997, p. 9, and *Independent on Sunday*, January 2, 1997.

39 Abu Zahr, *al-Watan al-'Arabi* (see above, note 35).

40 See *Reuters,* March 8, 1997. See also *Ha'aretz,* March 9, 1997.

41 See *AFP,* January 20, 1997, in *FBIS-Serial NC2001125597,* January 20, 1997; *Iran News,* January 7, 1997, in *FBIS-Serial LD1001210197,* January 7, 1997.

42 See *AFP,* January 10, 1997, in *FBIS-Serial NC1001131197,* January 10, 1997. The Mujahidin's attacks occurred in late December and early January. The mortar attack was launched on January 8.

43 From a report by Gen. J. H. Binford Peay, commander of U.S. Army Central Command, based on his interview with a well-informed new arrival from Baghdad; see *Washington Post,* January 29, 1997, p. A6; *Los Angeles Times,* January 10, 1997.

44 Saddam's problems within his tribe have also been augmented by problems with nontribal elements in Tikrit. For instance, in late 1992, U.S. officials met with Iraqi dissidents from Baghdad and Tikrit who sought help in toppling Sadam. News of the meeting leaked to Saddam's security forces and, in mid-July, the elderly Jasim Mukhlis and a number of senior army and Republican Guard officers from Tikrit, Baghdad, Mosul and other Sunni strongholds were arrested and later executed. Mukhlis was the scion of an important Tikriti family that managed to arrange for many Tikritis to be accepted at Iraq's military college and thus develop military careers. By executing him, Saddam

created a rift with important elements in his home town and in the army. See for example the interview with Sa'd Salih Jabr in *al-Wasat,* September 27–October 3, 1993; and *Guardian,* April 5, 1996.

45 See the interview with an expatriate Iraqi general, *Independent,* January 23, 1997. For details on the al-Haza' branch see Yunis al-Shaykh Ibrahim al-Samarra'i, *al-Qaba'il al-'Iraqiyya,* vol. II, (Baghdad: al-Sharq al-Jadid, 1989), p. 657. For a detailed family tree, see herein, pp. 22–23.

46 See al-Shaykh al-Samarra'i, *al-Qaba'il al-'Iraqiyya,* p. 658.

47 See *al-Hayat,* July 12, 1996.

48 All the available information indicates that the crash was a genuine accident ('Adnan was an inexperienced pilot who insisted on flying during a major sandstorm near Mosul). Still, owing to the supression of the investigation procedures, many in Iraq believe foul play was involved. Some believe that the assassin was Gen. Husayn Kamil, who wanted 'Adnan out of the way. See, for example, Jihad Salim from Nicosia, Cyprus, in *al-Watan al-'Arabi,* June 5, 1998, pp. 4–7.

49 Dr. Khashi' al-Mu'adidi, *Min Ba'd Ansab al-'Arab: A'ali al-Rafidayn* vol. II (Baghdad: University of Baghdad, Faculty of Education, 1990), pp. 216–217.

50 See Amatzia Baram, "Neo-Tribalism in Iraq: Saddam Husayn's Tribal Policies, 1991–1995," in *International Journal of Middle East Studies (IJMES)* 29 (February 1997), pp. 1–31; also relevant is an interview with Mish'an Rakkad al-Damin al-Jubburi, who named Guard officer Sattam Ghannam al-Jubburi as the ring-leader, in *al-Hayat* (London), August 18, 1995. Some of the most able Jubburi officers were temporarily restored to senior positions after the invasion of Kuwait, when the threat of war with the U.S.-led coalition forced Saddam to look to his most capable commanders. For instance, Lt. Gen. Sa'adi Tu'ma 'Abbas al-Jubburi was made minister of defense. General al-Jubburi was widely considered one of Iraq's greatest practitioners of defensive warfare, and his skillful defense of Basrah in 1982 when he was a corps commander had saved Iraq's second city from the first great Iranian offensive into Iraq.

51 Although the regime flatly denied that there had been an attempted coup d'état at the Abu Ghurayb garrison by Dulaymi army officers in mid-June 1995 (see *al-Jumhuriyya,* June 20, 1995; and *INA,* June 16, 1995, in *FBIS-NES-DR,* June 19, 1995, p. 22), it never denied the mid-May revolt at al-Ramadi. Indeed, by implication it even admitted it. See, for example, the admission to tribal shaykhs by the party boss in the Anbar (Dulaym) governorate, Muhammad Yunis Ahmad, that recently there were "conspiratorial plans and dirty and mean attempts to undermine the steadfastness of our . . . people," *al-Thawra,* May 28, 1995, in *FBIS-NES-*

DR, June 9, 1995, p. 45. One of al-Bu Nimr's shaykhs, Najib Humayd Farhan al-Ku'ud, admitted in May that there were "evildoers" and "idiots" in his tribe: see *INA,* June 28, 1995, in *FBIS-NES-DR,* June 29, 1995, p. 21. At least 170 people were killed and many arrested as a result of the revolt.

52 See *INA* newswire, May 7, 1996.

53 See an interview given by Maj. Gen. 'Abd al-Razzaq al-Jubburi of the Republican Guard, who defected in March 1991, to the Turkish newspaper *al-Mu'tamar,* November 8, 1996, p. 6. Also see the interview of Mish'an Jubburi in Helga Graham's article, *Independent on Sunday,* August 20, 1995.

54 Dale F. Eickelman, *The Middle East: An Anthropological Approach* (Englewood Cliffs, N.J.: Prentice Hall, 1989), p. 144. For more see Baram, "Neo-Tribalism in Iraq."

55 See the interview of Maj. Gen. 'Abd al-Razzaq al-Jubburi in *al-Mu'tamar,* and Graham, *Independent on Sunday.*

56 See, for example, the description by Maj. Gen. 'Abd al-Razzaq Sultan al-Jubburi of his coup attempt in 1994–1995, which involved a Dulaymi general and others, in *Corriere Della Sera,* September 11, 1996, in *FBIS-Serial BR1109101596,* September 11, 1996.

57 Two such revolts, both in the al-'Adl district—one in early March 1992, the other in January 1996—resulted in scores of casualties and hundreds of imprisonments.

58 See Baram, "Neo-Tribalism in Iraq."

Chapter 3

Party, Army, and Opposition: Domestic Support in Decline

The family quarrels that resulted in the defection of Husayn Kamil, coupled with the tribal frictions and several coup attempts, appear to have redounded, unexpectedly, to the benefit of the Ba'th party. Especially since May 1995, Saddam has been slowly reshaping Iraq's political structure (although not yet its internal security structure) to emphasize party ties and to break up the monopoly on political power previously enjoyed by his family and fellow tribesmen. Almost from the beginning of Ba'thist rule, Saddam's power base has been dominated by the old-time party faithful—mainly members of key Sunni tribes and nontribal Sunnis, but also Shi'is—selected military officers, and his closest relatives. At various points in his long rule, Saddam has favored different segments of this coalition when filling senior posts and enforcing his authority. Initially, while he was building his tribal coalition, he favored the Ba'th party. Yet, following the Gulf War, Saddam eased out party loyalists in favor of Iraqi military officers, his relatives, and members of the key Sunni tribes. In the early 1990s, the discovery of one coup plot after another led by members of important Sunni tribal allies—first the Jubbur, then the Ubayd, and finally the 'Dulaym—caused the further concentration of power in the hands of his extended family. The elevation of the family resulted ultimately in grave setbacks to the institutions they ran and to wide-ranging complaints of corruption, as well as in the bloody quarrels among the Ibrahims, the Majids, and 'Udayy, which in turn sparked Husayn Kamil's defection. Having seen the failure of this structure, Saddam once again reinvested power in the old party faithfuls who have the advantage of being less volatile and independent-minded than his own kin.

For example, Watban Ibrahim's replacement as interior minister was a long-time Ba'thist with a lengthy record of service to Saddam's regime. Muhammad Zimam 'Abd al-Razzaq al-Sa'dun is a Sunni Arab, born in 1942 in Suq al-Shuyukh—deep in the Shi'i south. He is also a member of the old and highly respected family of shaykhs, the Sa'duns of the Muntafiq. As a party old-timer, the new minister was acceptable to the party elite. By picking a Sunni with wide connections in the south, Saddam may have hoped the new minister would be acceptable to Sunnis and Shi'is alike. And as a scion of an important and very wealthy family under the monarchy, he is not a "black sheep," so he probably was acceptable to the upper social classes in Baghdad.[1]

'Ali Hasan al-Majid was similarly replaced as minister of defense by former Chief of Staff Sultan Hashim Ahmad, a professional military officer who is neither from Saddam's family, nor from his tribe, nor even from his region (false rumors spread by Iraqi expatriates notwithstanding).[2] General Hashim comes from a Sunni Arab family from Mosul and earned a distinguished reputation as a corps commander and member of the General Staff during the Iran–Iraq War. Saddam apparently chose him to assuage the army's officers corps, which reportedly had been offended by Saddam's choice of two of his cousins—first Husayn Kamil, then 'Ali Hasan al-Majid, neither of whom had any actual military credentials—as defense ministers after the Gulf War. By choosing Hashim, Saddam no doubt hoped to improve his standing in Mosul and among the large number of army and air force officers from Iraq's third most populous city. In view of the strenuous efforts by Iraqi opposition figures to try to recruit Muslawi officers, this is of particular importance.[3] Hashim was also chosen because Saddam was deeply impressed by his handling of the negotiations with Gen. Norman Schwarzkopf at Safwan at the end of the Gulf War. He never admitted defeat, and he extracted cease-fire terms that were very convenient for his government.

Similarly, the new chief of staff, Gen. 'Abd al-Wahid Shinan Aal Ribbat, the first Shi'i chief of staff of the modern Iraqi state, is also a party old-timer (he joined in the early 1960s). In addition, he was an appealing candidate to the president because he comes from a large tribe in the South (the Aal Ribbat), with whom Saddam still has very close ties. General Aal Ribbat conducted himself well as commander of the Iraqi VI Corps during the Gulf War and the subsequent *intifada* (uprising), when several of the units under his command proved instrumental in restoring order in Basrah immediately after the disastrous Iraqi defeat.

Finally, Saddam Husayn also dismissed a more distant paternal cousin, Kamil Yasin, from the position of deputy secretary general of the military bureau of the party (the president himself is the actual secretary general). The new deputy secretary general is Samir Najam, a Sunni Arab party old-timer who was Saddam's coconspirator in the unsuccessful attempt on Gen. 'Abd al-Karim Qasim's life in October 1959. Interestingly, the president has elevated another participant in the failed attack on Qasim—Hatim Hamdan al-'Azzawi—to a very prominent position, Secretary of the Presidential Office.

There have been other signs that Saddam is favoring old party friends over his relatives to fill high-profile political positions, though internal security positions have remained safely in the hands of family or tribe. In his communiqué denouncing Husayn Kamil for his betrayal, Saddam reminded his listeners of the old days of the Ba'th's underground activity before it took power, implying that only those who had gone through these hardships could understand how to rule.[4] This was a far cry from his speech on the Prophet's Birthday in 1991, when he invoked the Prophet's actions to legitimize his own blatant nepotism, or from his programmatic speech to the Extraordinary Meeting of the Tenth Regional Congress of the Ba'th party in October 1992, when he again cited the practices of the Prophet to justify elevating tribal leaders to positions of state leadership.[5] Similarly, after the defections, Saddam distributed Husayn Kamil's former positions to men who did not belong to either his family or his tribe.[6]

Another indication that Saddam Husayn has been leaning more heavily than before on his party comrades is his new political "kitchen cabinet" (as distinct from his military and internal security advisers), which consists of Vice President Taha Yasin Ramadan, Deputy Prime Minister Tariq 'Aziz, and the ministers of foreign affairs and information—all of them party old-timers—and also 'Ali Hasan al-Majid, as a reminder that the family has not been entirely excluded.[7] Yet, even 'Ali Hasan's inclusion in this group does not necessarily reflect a place for the family in Saddam's inner circle. Unlike Husayn and Saddam Kamil, or 'Udayy and Qusayy, 'Ali Hasan is not just family: He is also a party old-timer, having joined the Ba'th in 1960. As such, he can fill the most senior party positions without creating the impression of down-right nepotism.

The comeback of the party has also been apparent in a dramatic change in Saddam's public comments regarding the role of the party and the performance of party members. Before 1995, Saddam had been extremely critical of the party. During the intifada of March 1991, the party had performed miserably, especially in the Shi'i south. Many party members deserted their posts and sought refuge in the capital, leaving the southern towns to the rebels. Nor had they covered themselves in glory during the Gulf War: In Saddam's view, party members had been insufficiently supportive of the cause and had failed to instill the appropriate discipline and enthusiasm in the general population. After the Gulf War, Saddam castigated the party on several occasions in the most explicit and vitriolic fashion. He accused party members of being cowards, bad managers, isolated from the masses, and in pursuit of their own private agendas. He even criticized himself for having spared party members the experience of real battle during the Iran–Iraq War, which left them unready to combat the Shi'i uprising after the Gulf War. At that time, he warned that, if it were to continue on its present course, the party would lose its influence over state institutions and "its internal activity will stagnate."[8] As late as mid-1994, Saddam accused the party of "laxity and apathy."[9] *Babil*, too, was allowed to attack the party for losing "its old spirit," and party members for showing up at meetings only for their own private benefit. 'Udayy's newspaper went so far as to complain that certain party members who served as senior officials of the government were guilty of theft and bribery, and that the situation called "for electing the model official at the level of ministers, governors, . . . and institution heads . . . in accordance with the standard and principles contained in the Revolution . . . of the leader Saddam Husayn."[10] Although these attacks were doubtless part of an effort by 'Udayy to besmirch certain long-time party members (like Tariq 'Aziz) and replace them with his own cronies, they also reflected a wide-spread realization that the party was in such a steep decline that attacks against it would go unpunished.

Beginning in 1995, however, the party went from Saddam's whipping boy to his golden child. Saddam's central speech at the party's Eleventh Regional Congress in early July 1995 praised party members for their recovery, declaring that they were his most loyal supporters—more so than the army or the security apparatus.[11] Saddam praised the party's actions in the Shi'i south in countering guerrilla activities, its efforts to control commodities prices, and a litany of other achievements. Indeed, he felt confident enough in the party's support to deal it a new blow, announcing, as part of his "discovery" of Islam, that all members would now be forced to take the compulsory Qur'an courses. Since 1990, Saddam has introduced much Islamic rhetoric into his speeches, begun a widespread Islamic education campaign, and to some extent enacted the *shari'a*, or Islamic legal code. Some party members liked the change, but others—who were thoroughly secular—resented it. Saddam's new praise of the party seems genuine. He never hesitated to criticize the party when criticism was due, and there is no reason to doubt the sincerity of his adulation now. Since 1992 the press has regularly reported the efforts of party members in spreading the regime's messages, "refuting rumors," monitoring market prices, preventing illegal trade in foreign currency, and patrolling the streets against crime (*nawatir al-Sha'b*)—and all after their normal workdays, for very little, or no pay.[12] On the other hand, there have been reports from foreigners that these *nawatir* are not immune to bribery and the population continues to complain about the arbitrariness of many party officials. Saddam is aware of these complaints, but having no other tool, he will have to continue to rely on party members to perform these duties.[13]

Why has Saddam performed such a sudden turnabout on the level of political nominations, virtually returning to the regime's practices during its first years in power? One answer may be that Saddam has concluded that his cousins and half-brothers failed in their duties. From an outsider's perspective, this judgment is certainly correct. Watban could not curb a spreading crime wave in Iraq, endemic profiteering, or terrorist attacks in downtown Baghdad. Likewise, 'Ali Hasan al-Majid could not prevent widespread demoralization and massive desertions in the army (around 30 percent in many field units). He also was held responsible for Iraq's humiliating defeat at the hands of Talabani's Kurds on March 3, 1995, when Kurdish fighters battered the Iraqi Army around Irbil. But the sacking of family members went beyond just these two, suggesting that the problem is not the performance of specific relatives, but the problems created by the infighting among Saddam's family in general.

Again, the evidence points to a desire on Saddam's part to push his relatives further into the background and replace them, to a great extent, with party loyalists. Another sign of this shift was the emphasis on corruption that surfaced in Iraq at roughly the same time. This is particularly noteworthy because the massive corruption of Saddam's family was a major grievance of party members—closely tied, in their minds, with their having been shunted aside in favor of the tribal shaykhs and their sons.[14] Stories began to leak into the Iraqi press hinting at corruption in very high places—stories that Saddam had to have approved. For instance, the chairman of the Fiscal Control Bureau, Hikmat Mizban al-'Azzawi gave a long and detailed interview in which he discussed numerous cases of corruption in the government, including cases involving the "theft of tens of millions." Al-'Azzawi went on to identify the perpetrators as "high-ranking officials who may hold leadership-level jobs in the government" (read: cabinet ministers).[15] Following Watban's sacking, the National Assembly started a much-publicized anticorruption campaign aimed at his chief aides in the Interior Ministry, including four generals.[16] The terminology used could leave no room for doubt in the minds of the readers that Watban himself was either totally inept or corrupt. In another case, in the summer of 1995, Minister of Finance Ahmad Husayn Khudayr al-Samarra'i—the former head of the president's office—even divulged that in the past there were "numerous cases" when members of the president's family "transgressed [financially]," and that the president dealt with this corruption "harshly."[17] In the spring of 1996, Fadil Salfij al-'Azzawi, a first cousin on Saddam's mother's side, was removed as director of Iraq's General Intelligence (al-Mukhabarat al-'Amma). This was a rather straightforward case of excessive corruption and further demonstrated Saddam's desire to portray himself as a leader who does not succumb to nepotism.[18]

Most of these revelations came soon after the defection of the Kamils. For Saddam, this kind of criticism served multiple purposes: It let off steam, it neatly explained the Kamils' defection (al-Samarra'i argued that they knew Saddam would soon punish them for their "transgressions"), and it made it easier for him to remove some of his troublesome relatives from their powerful positions. In addition, relieving many of Saddam's family members became something of a necessity in mid-1995, as tensions within the family could easily have ignited outright violence between the forces of the Interior Ministry (the police, General Security, and other paramilitary units) and those of Saddam's sons—Qusayy's Special Republican Guard and 'Udayy's paramilitary Fida'iyyin.

The chastening of Saddam's family and the party members' own resurrection does not mean that the latter no longer have any grievances. They continue to feel marginalized by tribal shaykhs. The economic plight of many is so bad that the regime had to earmark 50 percent of all members' fees to establish a Party Fund (sunduq al-hizb) to assist the worst off of their number.[19] From time to time, even Saddam has felt the need to donate money to the fund to provide "a new incentive for work and inventiveness."[20] Members often complain about inept government officials who render useless their efforts to control prices. Finally, until recently, there was a feeling, especially among younger members, that they were destined to remain forever at the bottom of the party hierarchy. In the autumn of 1996, at a lecture in a research institute in the United States, this author commented that, since the late 1970s, members of the Regional Leadership, the party's highest body, have been people born no later than 1942 and who joined the party no later than the early 1960s. Secretaries of large party branches (*furu'*), small branches (*shu'bah*s) and divisions (*firqah*s) were still people born no later than 1944 and who joined the party no later than the mid-1960s. Even these people often complained that their advancement had been arrested unjustly, whereas the younger generation— those in their twenties, thirties, and even forties—had a much better reason for discontent: They generally have not reached even the level of secretary of *firqah*.[21] Then, in early 1997, Saddam Husayn himself addressed the problem of the aging, stagnating party leadership, by speaking of the need to "prepare young and able leaderships which will gradually take over from the [present] leaderships."[22] In the party's internal elections in September–October 1997, many midlevel party functionaries lost their positions to younger people, probably with the president's connivance. Saddam congratulated the ousted officials for their magnanimous spirit and the younger generation for having "injected new blood into the party's various echelons of leadership."[23]

It is still too early to tell how meaningful these various changes may be. Nevertheless, despite the generational frustration and reservations about some of Saddam's policies, the party appears to have regained its position as one of the regime's strongest bases of support. Unlike some senior party officials—such as former newspaper editor Sa'd Bazzaz—who were able to escape to the West, the vast majority of party members had no choice but to go on serving Saddam as best as they could. Their social position, their remaining financial rewards, and their very lives depend on the stability of the regime. During the Shi'i intifada of 1991, many party members were killed even after surrendering to the rebels.[24] This experience serves as a bitter lesson for all Ba'this. The party is a net asset to Saddam, and there are no signs that it is going to abandon him or that he is going to abandon it. For example, in his July 17, 1997, Revolution Day speech,

Saddam disappointed many in Iraq who expected him to announce steps toward political pluralism—including the legalization of some opposition parties. Had he done so, he would have struck a severe blow to the status of the Ba'th Party. Instead, he promised his citizens only more blood, sweat, and tears, and the continuation of the one-party system.

SADDAM, THE ARMY, AND THE REPUBLICAN GUARD

Saddam Husayn and the Ba'th have had a checkered history with the Iraqi armed forces. The Ba'th joined with the army to overthrow Qasim in 1963, only to be purged by the officers nine months after their successful coup. When the Ba'th regained power in July 1968, it was determined not to repeat its mistake. Before the military could move, the Ba'th purged Iraq's officer corps of its non-Ba'thi elements. Under Capt. (res.) Taha Yasin Ramadan, at least 2,000 senior and midlevel officers were cashiered for belonging to Nasserist or other opposition elements. Simultaneously, Ba'thi officers were promoted at a very rapid pace to ensure that committed party members held all senior military posts. Meanwhile, Ba'thi political officers were assigned to all major field commands and empowered to veto any decision made by the professional officers. Since then, Saddam has tended to see the army as a threat to his regime as much as an asset to his foreign policy. He monitors its activities closely, maintains numerous intelligence services and military units (such as the Republican Guard and the Special Republican Guard) as counterweights, screens promotions to senior ranks to ensure loyalty, and insists that the army leadership stay out of domestic politics.

Indeed, Saddam's animosity toward and fear of the military has manifested itself in the form of various insults and challenges to the officer corps over the course of his rule. On at least two occasions in the late 1970s, Saddam dared large gatherings of army and air force officers to try to topple the regime. He issued his challenges in the bluntest fashion—as only a former street thug could—thoroughly shocking his audience. Similarly, during the Iran–Iraq War, Saddam regularly humiliated his generals by blaming all of Iraq's military defeats on the officer corps. Saddam fired or executed commanders who had participated in unsuccessful operations— even if they were not to blame—to discourage the others from following their example. Meanwhile, he claimed all successes for himself. Like Stalin, toward the end of the war, Saddam had Iraq's papers refer less and less to his victorious generals (who by then had been boiled down to a fairly competent group of General Staff officers and senior field commanders largely responsible for the ultimate victory over Iran) and increasingly ascribe Iraqi victories to his own stewardship.

If his tight control and frequent humiliations of the military have been part of Saddam's stick, he has also offered it numerous carrots. Probably the most important of these has been the constant expansion and modernization of the armed forces. In part to appease the officer corps, the Ba'th embarked on a major program to strengthen Iraqi military forces. Soon after coming to power, the Ba'th regime introduced a new National Military Service Law that transformed the Iraqi Army: For the first time in Iraqi history, university graduates were subject to compulsory military service. At first they were required to serve for nine months, but in the mid-1970s this was increased to twelve, then eighteen, and then twenty-one months.[25] Following the Arab oil embargo in 1973–1974, and the dramatic increase in Iraqi oil revenues after the October War, Iraq greatly increased military spending to prepare for a confrontation with the Shah's Iran. At that time, the two states were locked in a bitter conflict over the Shatt al-Arab, support to the Kurds, and other issues. Ultimately, Iraq was forced to accept the Algiers Accord of 1975—essentially giving in to Iranian demands on the Shatt in return for an end to Iran's support for Kurds and Shi'is and minor territorial concessions that the Shah never fulfilled— because Baghdad concluded that it could not stand up to Iran's powerful, U.S.-equipped armed forces.

In response to the humiliation of the Algiers Accord, Iraq further accelerated its build-up to try to redress the military imbalance. Between 1975 and 1978, the Iraqi armed forces expanded from 155,000 to 362,000 while the Shah's army was cut down from 385,000 to 350,000. In 1980, as a result of Ayatollah Ruhollah Khomeini's revolution, Iran's standing forces dwindled to roughly 300,00 men, while Iraq's swelled to 430,000. Baghdad's military expenditures also expanded in leaps and bounds during this period. Between 1975 and 1978 they grew from $5.3 billion to $8.15 billion (in constant 1983 U.S. dollars). In 1980, Iraq's military expenditures reached $13.4 billion (in 1983 U.S. dollars).[26] In the meantime, in 1972 Iraq embarked on a project to build a nuclear weapon, which had it been successful would have been enormously prestigious for the Iraqi armed forces, raising them to the level of the superpowers and the handful of other nuclear states.[27] To the Iraqi officer corps, this rapid expansion and upgrading of the armed forces meant promotions, prestige, and a new status within Iraqi society. Moreover, once he took over the presidency, Saddam also introduced an elaborate system of economic rewards for successful officers, including plots of land, homes, cars and monetary gifts. All of these rewards were intended to ensure the loyalty of the officer corps and to compensate for the loss of their traditional political clout. But, in all probability, this military expansion was meant primarily to prepare for a confrontation with Iran. It certainly was not a purely defensive expansion, as suggested by some.[28]

After the crushing defeats inflicted on the Iraqi armed forces by Iran in 1981–1982, the officers finally realized that the militaristic spirit of their young president had devastating results for themselves and for Iraq. Yet, by then it was too late for them to do anything about it: The army was completely penetrated by Ba'thi officers and security agents, rendering a coup d'état nearly impossible. But the Iran–Iraq War also had a silver lining for Iraq's officers. As a result of Iran's relentless—if less than decisive—victories in 1982–1986, the Iraqi armed forces were repeatedly expanded to try to substitute quantity for their lack of quality. By the end of the war in 1988, Iraq boasted a staggering 1.5 million men in all of its various military and paramilitary services and it had become a nonconventional power as well. On April 2, 1990—the day Saddam threatened to "burn half of Israel" with chemical weapons—a Western reporter with long experience interviewing Iraqi generals found a consensus among the senior Iraqi officers that Saddam was a brilliant strategist. No matter how much they begrudged him, all considered him the first Arab leader who had managed to achieve strategic parity with Israel, and in so doing he had cut the Zionists down to size.[29]

Since the Gulf War, its attendant sanctions and embargoes, and the dismantling of most of Iraq's nonconventional weapons, these sentiments appear to have vanished. There is very little *targhib* (enticement) left in the Iraqi officer corps, and what remains is mostly *tarhib* (terror). For the most part, Iraq's soldiers harbor great resentment against the president, and no matter what Saddam's propagandists may claim, his officers fully understand what happened in the Gulf War. Saddam himself implied in certain postwar discussions with his officers that he was aware that some of them felt that the Iraqi army was forced to fight a formidable enemy against which they had no chance. For example, in one awards ceremony he tried to convince his officers, "We knew that the enemy would use against us sophisticated weapons . . . we prepared for it and studied these weapons like the Apache [helicopter gunship]." And he called upon his officers to tell their troops this "truth," rather than "lie" to them.[30] Saddam was evidently worried about his officers' loyalty, and in one meeting he jokingly suggested that he and they would stage a coup d'état against himself, so as "not to disappoint the West."[31] In an interview on Iraq's Army Day in 1992, then–Minister of Defense 'Ali Hasan al-Majid warned his officers against the efforts of the "Zionist entity," Iran, and "the reactionary Arab regimes" to incite them to treason.[32] A few months later, the chief of the military's Political Guidance Administration, Flight Brig. Gen. Jabbar Rajab Haddush, stressed the need for an "ideological army" (*jaysh 'aqa'idi*), and issued a booklet that explained the importance of being imbued with the party's faith and how an army officer could achieve it.[33] The fact that, twenty-five years after it took over in Baghdad, the Ba'th Party still felt the need to remind Iraqi officers that loyalty was important, suggests that something is very wrong.

The Iraqi Army today is hardly the force that smashed the Iranian armed forces in 1988 and overran Kuwait in thirty-six hours in 1990. Its strength remains impressive on paper; although its numbers have declined from more than one million soldiers at the start of the Gulf War to around 400,000 today, and from sixty-six to twenty-three divisions, it is still a very large army. In addition, the Iraqis have maintained the same rigorous tempo of training they observed before the Gulf War (although there is little evidence that Iraqi training methods have improved significantly).[34] Nevertheless, there are tremendous problems at all levels of the Iraqi military. The army is short of everything from tanks, artillery pieces, ammunition, and spare parts, to rations, uniforms, and shoes. Saddam has repeatedly purged distinguished senior officers, many of them war heroes from the Iran–Iraq War, for suspected disloyalty. The army must contend with daily guerilla raids in the South and skirmishes with the Kurds in the North— neither of which it is able to handle as it would like because of the restrictions imposed on its actions by the United Nations. After the Gulf War, when the remaining weapons holdings were redivided among the force, much of the best equipment in the Iraqi inventory went to the Republican Guard, exacerbating the resentment and demoralization of the regular army's officer corps. Finally, the systematic efforts of the United Nations Special Commission (UNSCOM) to uncover and destroy Iraq's arsenal of ballistic missiles and chemical, biological, and nuclear weapons has been another source of frustration for the Iraqi armed forces.[35]

These various problems have badly undermined the morale of the military. Between March 1991 and mid-1996 there were no less than three military coup d'état attempts. All failed, but given the pervasiveness of Saddam's security forces—and the horrible fate of failed assassins in Iraq—the fact that army officers have mounted at least three serious attempts against Saddam in recent years demonstrates the extent of their frustration and disillusionment. Moreover, the regime has grown increasingly disturbed by more ethereal phenomena. Almost two years after the Gulf War the RCC issued a strange decree stipulating that any military man proven to be "disloyal to the rule of the [Ba'th] Revolution and its principles" will be punishable by forced retirement or demotion.[36] This edict was aimed at curbing expressions of discontent and loose talk in general, indicating that the regime had become so concerned about the morale of the military that it was trying to forbid grumbling in the ranks. Desertion rates remain staggeringly high and are a major reason Baghdad repeatedly has had to reduce the number of divisions on its order of battle. Despite these efforts, few units in the army can boast above 65 percent to 70 percent of their authorized manpower. As another sign of this problem, even the air force has been forced to accept recruits with much lower matriculation grades than ever before. In the past, the minimum requirement for the Iraqi Air Force academy had been an average of 80, but the air force had to lower it to 60 in 1996 to find enough suitable candidates. The situation is so bad that widespread rumors in Baghdad suggest Saddam has instructed Qusayy—with the assistance of 'Izzat Ibrahim al-Duri, Samir 'Abd al-'Aziz Najam, and several internal security officials—to carry out a sweeping reorganization. Reportedly, Qusayy will pension off many regular army officers; disband additional low-quality army units; and place the army, air force, Republican Guard, *Quwat al-Tawari'* (emergency forces), *Fida'iyyi-Saddam* (Saddam's would-be martyrs), Himaya, and the military industry forces under a unified command.[37]

Given this state of affairs, what is noteworthy is that there have not been more coup attempts. Saddam's sham democratic façade notwithstanding, Iraq is still the most brutal dictatorship in the Middle East and raw fear still reigns supreme. In Saddam's Iraq, not only the rebellious but even his own family are put to the sword without the slightest hesitation or remorse. Any group of army officers that decides to roll the dice and try to topple the regime must find a way through the seemingly impenetrable wall of security and military forces that protects Saddam. As described by military analyst Michael Eisenstadt, the capital is defended by the heavily armed and fanatically loyal battalions of the Special Republican Guard.[38] Baghdad is further surrounded by the three most powerful divisions of the Republican Guard—the Hammurabi, Madina al-Munawrah, and al-Nida armored divisions, which are superior to any of the regular army divisions in terms of proficiency, equipment, and morale.[39] A revolt in the army would also be at a disadvantage in terms of command and control. A handful of divisions attempting to overthrow the government would inevitably lack the communications, transportation, and other coordination mechanisms available to the well-organized Guard units. The Guard is a self-sufficient force in every respect: It has all necessary supporting arms; it has its own communications and logistics sytems; and it does not report to Iraq's military high command, but directly to the Presidential Palace—in the person of Qusayy Saddam Husayn. These features make it a highly effective regime-protection force. The chances of an army unit penetrating this ring of steel are slim and this knowledge undoubtedly has deterred many would-be coup-makers.

For Iraq's officer corps, fear of failure is combined with a lack of political experience as a disincentive for moving against the president. Unlike the Syrian case, for example, the Iraqi Army has been politically emasculated over the last thirty years and thus the decision to intervene in politics in any form requires crossing important psychological barriers as well. Moreover, Saddam has not completely lost his ability to provide carrots to the military. In particular, he plays on the chords of Iraqi national honor, presenting Iraq as the only Arab state to resist U.S. domination. More tangibly, he has been doing his best to convince his army officers that Iraq has not lost its nonconventional arsenal and the prestige they bring. This is one of the causes of his remarkable intransigence toward the UN inspectors, a stubborness that, by 1998, had cost Iraq roughly $120 billion in lost oil revenues.

The problems causing discontent in the army have even affected the Republican Guard, raising the spectre of a coup by the Guard itself. The Guard remains better off than the regular army in every way, but there are growing signs of difficulties here too. Although the Special Republican Guard still enjoys all of its customary perks and is still very well-equipped and well-supplied, the rest of the Guard has felt the pinch of sanctions. Many Guard units have been forced to accept older equipment to replace weapons lost during the Gulf War, and even the Guard formations have seen their authorized strengths slashed because of Iraq's severe equipment shortages. Between January 1996 and mid-1997, when oil revenues began to flow back into Iraq after Saddam's belated acceptance of UN Security Council Resolution 986, some Guard formations have even been disbanded. Guard salaries have not fully kept pace with inflation, while bonuses and other gifts have dwindled (although the Guard still does much better than the army on all of these counts). When combined with an inflationary crisis in 1996 (see below), these problems sent tremors through the Guard.

Of course, Saddam is not ignorant of the possibility of a threat from the Guard, and his precautions—coupled with the greater loyalty and privileges of the Guard—make coup attempts from this quarter even less likely than from the regular army. At least since January 4, 1990, when the Jubbur coup was exposed and found to include officers from the Guard, Saddam has taken steps to insulate himself against a move from within this organization. The expansion of the Special Republican Guard, the Special Security Organization, and other regime-protection forces was one response. Another was the establishment of Fida'iyyi-Saddam on October 7, 1994 under 'Udayy's command.[40] At first the *Fida'iyyin* had no uniform, and its equipment was laughable: Members carried a random assortment of rifles and sub-machine-guns, and their only heavy weapons were Soviet-made PT-76s—obsolete amphibious tanks. In June 1996, at the same time that a new coup plot was exposed in both the Guard and the Special Guard, the regime increased its efforts to recruit young men for the Fida'iyyin corps.[41] By early 1997, the Fida'iyyin had been upgraded in every respect. It is still no match for the Guard, but coupled with the Special Guard, it is acting as a counter-weight to it.

Saddam's unmasking of the Republican Guard coup attempt of June 1996 was yet another sign of the continuing efficiency of his internal security system. The plot was uncovered at least two months before the revolutionaries planned to act, and it appears that the security system was simply waiting for the right moment to strike. Nevertheless, the details of the plot must have been troubling for Saddam. First, the regime made at least 100 arrests, although there appear to have been only seven to ten executions. Second, those executed were dangerously well-placed.[42] They were not senior officers, but operational-level field-grade officers who, if not exposed, might actually have pulled off a coup d'état. They included one brigadier general (a Tikriti no less), one colonel, one lieutenant colonel, and one captain—all from fighting units of the Republican Guard and Special Republican Guard—plus a lieutenant colonel from the Guard's Department of Political Guidance, an air force colonel stationed at al-Rashid air base in Baghdad, and a major from the Guard's intelligence staff. Another brigadier general and two junior officers from the infantry may also have been executed.[43] The security authorities were so worried that they even arrested Lt. Gen. Hamid Sha'ban, a pilot, adviser to Saddam, former commander of the air force, and member of al-Bu Nasir.[44] His name had surfaced during the interrogation of the would-be revolutionaries, who had considered him a potential figurehead once Saddam was out of the way. General Sha'ban was eventually released,[45] but his arrest and interrogation demonstrate that even eminent members of the president's own tribe are no longer above suspicion.

The failed 1996 attempt was at least the second time that Republican Guard officers have been involved in a coup d'état attempt since 1990. Saddam considers such episodes so dangerous that they have been contributory factors to some of his biggest military adventures. In 1990, the Jubburi plot probably contributed to Saddam's decision to solve his postwar economic and political problems by invading Kuwait. In 1996, the Republican Guard plot appears to have contributed to his decision to launch the September 1996 offensive against Irbil, in Iraqi Kurdistan. Specifically, Saddam needed to give the Guard a victory. He needed to prove to his officers that he still had both the courage to defy the Americans and the viciousness to settle the account with Jalal Talabani, which had been open since the Iraqi Army's humiliation by Talabani's Kurds in March 1995. In short, Saddam urgently needed to prove to his officers that he was still a "manly" warrior. With the political help of Mas'ud Barzani's Kurds, Saddam managed to achieve both goals.[46] As opposed to his claimed victory over the United States in the Gulf War, this time the regime's claims, although still wildly exaggerated, had a more realistic ring to them. Baghdad trumpeted that the Iraqi flag "flies high," while the American flag flew "at half staff."[47]

Iraq paid a price for the attack on Irbil, mainly by having to succumb to the U.S. decision to expand the no-fly zone over southern Iraq. Yet, on the whole, the operation strengthened Saddam. If nothing else, it elevated his standing with the Guard and probably with the army as well. Furthermore, the victory in Irbil freed his hands to accept Resolution 986. Having proved his mettle, having humiliated Talabani and the United States, having eliminated the Iraqi opposition and U.S. intelligence personnel in

Kurdistan, and having secured a victory, however small, for the Guard, he could afford the limited humiliation involved in accepting a UN resolution that he had previously rejected as incompatible with Iraq's sovereignty. Moreover, once the oil started to flow, he could then start a war of attrition against the UN monitoring teams, which he did during the summer of 1997, escalating to a full-blown crisis in October of that year.

THE OPPOSITION

No less than thirty organizations actively oppose the Iraqi Ba'th regime. Most are tiny, often consisting of less than ten people. Many of these smallest groups are based in Damascus. Others are the successors of organizations that have existed since the monarchy—such as the two Communist opposition parties and the opposition Ba'th party that favors the Syrian "branch" of the Ba'th. The main opposition groups, however, tend to fall into three broad categories: ethnic, religious, and secular-nationalist. The main ethnic opposition groups are the two major Kurdish militias, the Kurdish Democratic Party (KDP) and the Patriotic Union of Kurdistan (PUK). The former has been fighting the central government of Iraq—though under a different flag, the personal-tribal flag of the mullah Mustafa Mas'ud al-Barzani—off and on since 1943. Jalal Talabani's PUK turned against the government during the Iraq–Iraq War. The main religious opposition groups are Shi'i organizations that claim to speak for the whole Iraqi population, but in their propaganda they target mainly their coreligionists in Baghdad and southern Iraq. Finally, the principal secular nationalist organization is the Iraq National Congress (INC), an umbrella organization whose purpose is to try to coordinate all of the various opposition activities, but which also has dedicated operatives of its own.

Of the religious opposition groups, the most important are a trio of Shi'i organizations. All three are based in Iran but have important liaison and support elements in the West.

The most active of the three is the Supreme Assembly of the Islamic Revolution in Iraq (SAIRI), which was established in 1982 under Iranian auspices. It is currently led by the Najaf-born, Tehran-based Ayatollah Muhammad Baqir al-Hakim, the son of Iraq's former chief Shi'i authority, Muhsin al-Hakim, who died in 1970. SAIRI is by far the best-financed and largest of the Shi'i opposition groups (numbering around 3,000–4,000 fighters). During the March 1991 Shi'i intifada, SAIRI sent several hundred armed insurgents into Iraq to aid the uprising, the largest contingent of all the groups. In the Shi'i areas of Iraq, SAIRI can count on fairly extensive support, mainly from those who remember Hakim's father. Any new large-scale Shi'i revolt seems a distant possibility, but guerrilla warfare is certainly an option, and some of it is indeed being supported by SAIRI.

The Islamic Da'wa Party of Iraq is the oldest of the three, having been founded in 1957. The Da'wa is a much smaller organization than SAIRI but is more closely knit. Da'wa members are highly disciplined and have active intelligence and sabotage cells in many parts of Iraq, including Baghdad. Yet, according to interviews with Da'wa members in the West, the party was badly demoralized by the regime's victorious assault on Irbil in August–September 1996.

The last and least well known of the three Shi'i groups is 'Amal, the Islamic Action Organization. It was established in Karbala in the 1960s by the illustrious Shirazi clergy family and is run today by their cousins, the Mudarrisis. It numbers a few hundred members.[48]

Over the last thirty years, two rival militias have dominated the Kurdish opposition to Baghdad. Barzani's KDP dominates Kurdistan north and west of a line running roughly from Irbil to Dukan. Talabani's PUK rules most of southern and eastern Iraqi Kurdistan. From 1991 to 1994, largely through U.S. efforts, the PUK and the KDP maintained a tense truce that enabled them to hold elections and establish a joint administrative system based on a parliament and autonomous local government. But the deep mistrust and competition between the two camps did not subside. Major bones of contention—such as control over Irbil (mostly in Talabani's hands, but contested by the KDP), and finances (Talabani demanded an equal share in the revenues accruing from the semilegal deliveries of Iraqi oil into Turkey)—have also fueled tensions. In 1994, this precarious system collapsed and hostilities resumed. Talabani sought aid from Iran, which provided some money, weapons, training, logistical support, and, at least for a few days in 1996, Iranian Revolutionary Guardsmen. This Iranian backing, although limited, partially explains Talabani's victories against Barzani's forces during the summer of 1996. Indeed, that August, Barzani became so fearful that Iranian support for Talabani would lead to his defeat that he "made a pact with the devil": He invited Saddam to help him beat back the PUK. The result was a major military achievement for the KDP and a major political victory for Saddam. Iraqi troops smashed the PUK forces in Irbil and allowed the KDP to drive Talabani's troops into a small enclave in the mountains around Sulaymaniyya. Barzani's alliance with Saddam dealt a major blow to the idea of an autonomous Kurdistan, destroyed the INC network in northern Iraq, and undermined British and U.S. interests in Iraq. Moreover, Barzani was unable to drive the PUK out of Iraq altogether, and Talabani's forces quickly regrouped and re-armed for the next round of fighting. Eventually, the Clinton administration was able to exert enough pressure on both sides to patch up their differences, which produced a partial agreement and a cease-fire later that year.[49]

Kurdish unity suffered yet another setback when Turkey launched a massive intervention into Iraqi Kurdistan in October 1997. Ankara's forces have conducted counterinsurgency operations in Iraq against the anti-Turkish guerillas of the Kurdistan Workers' Party (PKK) with or without Baghdad's consent, for more than a decade. Yet, the October 1997 incursion was unusually large and penetrated unusually deep into Iraqi Kurdistan. Turkish goals were the same as always—extirpate the PKK bases there— but this time they were actively assisted by the KDP. For its part, the PUK accused Turkey of making common cause with the KDP against them, and even claimed that Turkish forces had deliberately bombed PUK positions. (Unlike the KDP, the PUK has always been reluctant to fight the their fellow Kurds in the PKK). On October 13, 1997, the PUK resumed combat operations against the KDP.[50] These were the first clashes in almost a year and they became exceptionally violent, with particularly fierce battles at the strategic locations of Shaqlawa, north of Irbil, and Haj 'Umran.[51] On October 17 a new cease-fire was agreed upon, only to dissolve quickly in renewed fighting. Talabani's forces agreed to withdraw to their original positions, but only in return for an equal status in the regional capital, Irbil, and an equal share in smuggled oil revenues.[52] These conditions were unacceptable to Barzani, who opted instead to keep fighting. Meanwhile, there have been reliable reports that Talabani in turn has opened a dialogue with Saddam to try to split the regime from the KDP.

These events make clear that the rancorous Kurdish infighting and the ordeal of the Kurdish people is far from over. As a result of the combination of the Iraqi army's atrocities in Iraqi Kurdistan in 1988–1991 and the inter-Kurdish fighting, by late 1997 one-third of the region's three million inhabitants were internal refugees. Although the fighting itself has been one cause of this problem, another is that both Talabani and Barzani regularly deport people they suspect of sympathies toward the rival camp.[53] Meanwhile, American damage-control efforts since the fall of Irbil have enjoyed some success. Since November 1997, the KDP and the PUK have been talking rather than shooting at each other. Nevertheless, without full implementation of the power-sharing arrangement roughly along the lines of the Ankara agreement they are bound to fail over the longer term.

Autonomous Kurdistan cannot sustain another blow like that of August–September 1996. New, widespread infighting will likely draw in Iran and Turkey to support opposite camps. Renewed fighting will also present Saddam with additional opportunities to intervene again, this time probably more decisively. Under such circumstances, a takeover by Baghdad is a real possibility. If given a pretext, Saddam could try to retake the North, and considering the unpopularity of the September 1996 U.S. military reprisal against the attack on Irbil, it is unclear whether the United States or any other outside power will have the political will to stop Saddam. Not only would this constitute a catastrophic defeat for the Kurds, but it would also represent a resounding comeback for Saddam. Judging by the state of affairs in Kurdistan in late 1997, another possibility exists—namely, that Saddam will be called back by both Kurdish factions. At the moment both Barzani and Talabani are negotiating with him.[54] In the meantime, Saddam can harass Barzani by supporting the anti-Turkish PKK—which is having turf battles with Barzani's militia—and he can also harass Talabani, though by more direct means. Either way, a return to Kurdistan would undoubtedly strengthen Saddam's standing with his mostly Sunni Arab power base, as well as his image in the Arab world. Thus if the Kurdish war starts again, the dream of true autonomy for Iraqi Kurds will be lost for a very long time. On the other hand, a stable Kurdistan—one with a meaningful presence of other opposition groups, like the INC—could serve as a model for the rest of Iraq.

Turning to the secular–nationalist opposition, the most important of these organizations is the liberal Iraq National Congress, led by a London- and Kurdistan-based businessman, Dr. Ahmad Chalabi. Although in principle the INC is an umbrella organization, in practice it functions as an opposition group in its own right. Before the September 1996 Irbil crisis the INC had several hundred activists and a sophisticated communications and information-gathering center in Salah al-Din, in Iraqi Kurdistan. They carried out continuous and highly useful intelligence-gathering activities, as well as psychological warfare operations, throughout Iraq. Perhaps their finest hour came in March 1995, when they joined with Jalal Talabani's PUK to launch a large offensive against Saddam's troops around Irbil.

Thanks to good field intelligence and complete surprise, the combined INC–PUK forces managed to rout two Iraqi army brigades. Their plan had also included a simultaneous revolt in the Shi'i south and a military coup d'état in Baghdad, and although both of these never occured, their victories in Kurdistan were still a humiliating defeat for Saddam.[55]

Since their success in March 1995, the INC's fortunes have mostly soured. The Iraqi assault on Irbil the next year—and the broader offensive by Mas'ud Barzani's Kurdish Democratic Party (KDP) which followed—wiped out most of the INC bases in Kurdistan. After they regained control of Irbil, Saddam's *mukhabarat* (intelligence service) reportedly executed more than ninety INC cadres on the spot and took many others as prisoners. According to PUK sources, they understood that there would be U.S. military action against an Iraqi offensive. But this is not what the then–assistant secretary of state for Near Eastern affairs, Robert Pelletreau, actually promised. Whereas he could not recall his precise words in his telephone conversation with Talabani on the eve of the offensive, Pelletreau insisted that he did not give a commitment for U.S. military involvement to prevent or to counter the Iraqi assault. He was not in the position to do this, because by then "no decision was made." At the same time, he did convey to Talabani that the United States "was not walking away."[56] The United States did punish Saddam by launching a few cruise missiles aganist his surface-to-air batteries and by extending the no-fly zone, and the United States remained engaged in Kurdistan, but the damage was great. Today the INC has rebuilt part of its network in the north, but only in the PUK-controlled areas around Sulaymaniyya. Yet even this presence is in jeopardy, as Talabani has opened a dialogue with Baghdad and already asked the INC to evacuate his territories.[57] The INC has even lost its crucial role as mediator and observer of the on-again off-again truce between the KDP and the PUK, having surrendered this function to a new force of non-Kurdish northerners trained by the Turks and financed by the United States.

The second most important secular opposition organization is the National Accord (*al-Wifaq al-Watani*), which until recently operated from Amman. The Wifaq boasts numerous ex-Ba'thi and ex-army officers as members and its activities have largely focused on the leverage these men and their contacts in the party and the armed forces bring. The Wifaq's last and so far most conspicuous operation was an attempt to engineer a military coup d'état in August 1996 through its contacts in Baghdad. Unfortunately, Saddam's mukhabarat uncovered the plot and snuffed it out in June–

July 1996.

The failure of the Wifaq coup attempt has become an all-too-predictable pattern, as Saddam's mukhabarat always seems to be one step ahead of the opposition. At least since January 1989, every coup d'état attempt has been exposed and eliminated with great ferocity well before the plotters were set to act. In every case the mukhabarat had a very accurate warning of the plot and simply waited for the right moment to pounce on the would-be revolutionaries. The system works so well essentially because of Saddam's combination of the carrot and the stick: Internal security officers are lavishly rewarded for carrying out their duties successfully but are also severely punished for mistakes. A security officer who neglects his duty can expect summary execution.[58] This way Saddam keeps his guards in a state of constant anxiety. Previous efforts to topple the regime have also demonstrated that the larger the group involved, and the more closely connected it is with bodies outside of Iraq, the more it becomes likely the plot will be exposed. Some of the opposition groups clearly do not have the right contacts in the army, the Republican Guard, the Special Republican Guards, and the Special Security necessary to pull off a successful coup, and those that do invariably have been penetrated by Saddam's internal security. Consequently, the efforts of the various opposition groups to overthrow the regime have failed, as far as internal coup attempts are concerned.

Not all opposition-led attacks on the regime need be destined for failure, though such an outcome would be likely in the present climate. The March 1995 INC–PUK offensive caught the regime by surprise and resulted in a major propaganda victory, although the effort to raise a nationwide revolt that was intended to accompany this assault—ostensibly a march on Mosul—failed to gain the backing of the United States or Barzani's KDP. Had these two components been added to the mix, its chances of success would have been better. Moreover, assassination attempts against Saddam and his family by tiny groups and including well-placed individuals from the internal security services, ruling family, and al-Bu Nasir tribe have enjoyed much greater success than large coup attempts. The best example of this was the nearly successful attempt on 'Udayy's life on December 12, 1996, which was conducted by no more than five people, all of whom escaped after doing serious harm to Saddam's favorite son. In another instance, assassins hid a large explosive device inside a tractor abandoned by the side of a road that was detonated as Saddam's convoy passed by on December 28, 1993. Saddam was saved by sheer luck. Several days later, a lone Guard officer opened fire on the president.[59] In addition, various opposition groups have been able to set off bombs in downtown Baghdad from time to time, killing and wounding innocent passersby.[60] When directed against civilians, however, these attacks are counterproductive. Not only are such attacks immoral, but they present the opposition as murderous. Similar attacks, however, when directed against sensitive targets—not including government ministries and newspaper headquarters—could have a profound effect on the regime's morale.

Because of the repeated failure of attacks on Saddam, the main role of the INC and other opposition groups, for now, is merely to keep the flame of rebellion flickering. Their continued existence serves as a reminder to the international community and to their countrymen still inside Iraq that the Ba'th regime is illegitimate and at least some Iraqis are willing to openly oppose Saddam Husayn's rule. Further down the line, following methodical preparations and, possibly, an American dialogue with additional opposition groups that are ready to commit themselves to a democratic agenda, the INC and the opposition in general may still play a much more decisive role.

NOTES

1 See *Republic of Iraq Radio Network*, May 22, 1995, in *Foreign Broadcast Information Service–Near East and South Asia–Daily Report (FBIS-NES-DR)*, May 23, 1995, p. 26.

2 See *Iraqi TV*, July 18, 1995, in *FBIS-NES-DR*, July 19, 1995, p. 31.

3 See Gen. Wafiq al-Samarra'i in *London Iraqi Broadcasting Corporation Press Release in Arabic*, December 16, 1994, in *FBIS-NES*, December 20, 1994, p. 23.

4 See *Iraqi TV*, August 11, 1995, in *FBIS-NES-DR*, August 14, 1995, pp. 25–27.

5 For Saddam's speech on the Birthday of the Prophet, see *al-Jumhuriyya*, September 21, 1991, in *FBIS-NES*, September 26, 1991, pp. 21–23. For his speech to the Extraordinary Session of the Tenth Regional Congress, see "Last Part of Saddam's Speech to Ba'th Congress," *Republic of Iraq Radio Network*, October 7, 1992, in *FBIS-NES*, October 8, 1992, p. 15.

6 'Adnan 'Abd al-Majid Jasim moved from his post as deputy chief of the Presidential Office to take over as Minister of Industry and Minerals. The acting director of the Military Industrialization Organization, General Engineer

'Amir Muhammad Rashid, was appointed oil minister. Rashid is a German-educated engineer turned general and a bureacurat without a party record of any significance. He had been Kamil's chief aid before the defection. See *Iraqi TV*, August 10, 1995, in *FBIS-NES*, August 11, 1995, p. 18.

7   See *INA*, August 24, 1995, in *FBIS-NES-DR*, August 25, 1995, p. 41.

8   See Saddam's speech at the Tenth Extraordinary Congress, *Republic of Iraq Radio Network in Arabic*, October 7, 1992, in *FBIS-NES*, October 8, 1992, pp. 16–19; and at the Tenth Regional Congress in mid-September 1991, as reported in the Iraqi TV and radio, September 15, 1991, in *FBIS-NES-DR*, September 16, 1991, pp. 20ff; and a speech to members of party *furu' tanzimat al-hizb* (branches) leadership in Baghdad, in *al-Jumhuriyya*, November 24, 1992.

9   See *Republic of Iraq Radio Network*, June 6, 1994, in *FBIS-Serial 0806192094*, June 8, 1994.

10   Muzhir 'Arif, *Babil*, November 13, 1993, in *FBIS-NES-DR*, November 13, 1994, pp. 5–7.

11   See *Iraqi TV*, July 14, 1995, in *FBIS-NES-DR*, July 18, 1995, pp. 33–34.

12   See Saddam's instructions in this regard in his speech to the Baghdad party *Tanzimat*, in *al-Jumhuriyya*, November 24, 1992, p. 3. See also in that article instructions to party members on how to prevent corruption, how to make sure judges are not too lenient on thieves and robbers, and other assignments. For information on the authority vested in the party's branches, including to close shops for six months or permanently if they are found profiteering; and to detain their owners for six months to one year in party facilities, see *Republic of Iraq Radio Network*, June 2, 1994, in *FBIS-Serial 0206210694*, June 2, 1994. For the authority of any *shu'bah* (small branch) to decide by majority vote to detain any buyer or seller of foreign currency outside the officially approved system for one to five years, and to refer extreme cases to a civil court that could sentence the offender to amputation of the right hand and left leg, see *al-Thawra*, June 24, 1994.

13   For example, see *al-Majd*, August 11, 1997, reporting his promise to rein-in party officials.

14   See, for example, As'ad Hamud al-Sa'dun, *Babil*, November 1, 1993; Dr. Yusuf Hamdan, *al-Thawra*, October 15, 1992. Reports of the graft in Saddam's family are now widespread. No one inside Iraq can afford to make such accusation openly, but several highly respected senior Iraqi exiles, after their defections, have described the illicit dealings of Saddam's relatives. See, for example, four-star general and former Chief of Staff Nizar al-Khazraji, reporting that 'Ali Hasan al-Majid is nicknamed "The Thief of Baghdad," in *al-Hayat*, April 16, 1996, in *FBIS-NES-DR*, April 18, 1996, p. 25.

15 See *Alif Ba'*, October 4, 1995, in *FBIS-NES-DR*, January 17, 1996, pp. 49–53. See also discussion of corruption in the administration, even though not in the context of the president's family, *Alif Ba'*, February 1, 1995, pp. 18–19, in *FBIS-NES-DR*, April 26, 1995, pp. 29–31.

16 See *al-'Iraq*, November 28 and 30, 1995.

17 See the interview of Ahmad Husayn al-Samarra'i in *al-Quds al-'Arabi*, September 11, 1995, as quoted in *al-Malaff al-'Iraqi*, no. 46 (October 1995), p. 35.

18 Because of inside information he had advance warning of the intention to start negotiations with the UN over Resolution 986. Expecting the Iraqi dinar to recover once this became public knowledge, he lent large sums of money in worthless dinars. When the dinar gained in value overnight following the announcement of the impending negotiations, he demanded his money back in suddenly valuable dinars. Saddam made him an example, dismissed him, and placed him under house-arrest.

19 Saddam's speech at the Tenth Extraordinary Congress, *Republic of Iraq Radio Network*, October 7, 1992, in *FBIS-NES*, October 8, 1992, pp. 16–19.

20 For example, he gave ID 1 million to *far' Maysan* in the south; see *al-Thawra*, July 14, 1993.

21 See Amatzia Baram, "Saddam's Iraq," *PolicyWatch* (Washington, D.C.: The Washington Institute for Near East Policy, September 12, 1996), p. 2. The information on members of the party's regional leadership is based on the author's own research, to be published soon. The information on the lower echelons of party cadres is based on an unpublished master of arts dissertation by Ronen Zeidel, "The Iraqi Baath Party, 1948–1995: Personal and Organizational Aspects," supervised by Amatzia Baram and presented to the University of Haifa, August 1997.

22 Saddam to cabinet ministers in a televised speech, May 26, 1997, as quoted by *al-Malaff al-'Iraqi*, no. 66 (June 1997), p. 4; the speech was also translated in *FBIS-NES-DR 97–146*, May 26, 1997.

23 See *INA*, October 9, 1997, in *FBIS-NES-DR97–282*, October 9, 1997.

24 Author's interview with four Shi'i rebels who participated in the intifada, May 5–8, 1994. See also Kanan Makiya, *Cruelty and Silence: War, Tyranny, Uprising, and the Arab World* (New York: W. W. Norton, 1993), pp. 68–72.

25 An interview with "'Umar," who served in the army for a few years during the Iran–Iraq War. See also Law 65 of 1969, in *al-Jumhuriyya*, May 15, 1969. In reality, only a very few were actually *released* from military service after 1975. Initially, Saddam kept them in uniform under the pretext of an imminent Israeli threat, but they then got caught in the series of Iraqi national

emergencies—the Iran–Iraq War, the Gulf War, and the post-Gulf War confrontations with the United States—during which Saddam retained many men under arms.

26   U.S. Arms Control and Disarmament Agency, *World Military Expenditures and Arms Transfers 1986* (Washington, D.C.: U.S. Government Printing Office, 1986), pp. 79, 121.

27   Author interview with an Israeli intelligence officer who served in 1972 and dealt with Iraq; Israel, 1989.

28   For a theory, developed as late as 1987, in which the military expenditure and expansion were said to be for purely defensive purposes, see Efrayim Karsh, *The Iraq–Iran War: A Military Analysis* (London: Chatham House, 1987), p. 7.

29   Author interview with a Dutch reporter who spent three weeks in Iraq in April 1990; Israel, May 1990.

30   See *INA* newswire, March 2, 1992. Decorated officers assured the president that they had, indeed, been ready for the Gulf War; see *al-Jumhuriyya*, March 11, 1992. In one story, he recollected that, before the Gulf War, a Guard officer complained to him that there was no information on the Apache. He then sent him to Gen. Muhammad 'Abd al-Qadir, the assistant chief of staff for training, to receive a study of the helicopter gunship that Saddam "had compelled him to prepare" years beforehand, and a joint committee of the Ministry of Defense and the Guard was set up to work out the tactics; see *al-'Iraq*, March 3, 1992. For the officers, this must have been a very disturbing report: Clearly, the information was not readily available to the units, and they never trained accordingly.

31   See *al-'Iraq*, December 15, 1991.

32   See *INA* newswire, January 6, 1992.

33   See *al-Thawra*, January 6, 1993.

34   See a report by a senior U.S. military officer in the *Washington Post*, January 29, 1997, p. A6.

35   Interview with a senior official in UNSCOM, New York, October 1995.

36   See *Babil*, November 22, 1992.

37   See, for example, *Sawt al-Mar'a*, February 19, 1997, in *Gulf 2000* (an internet discussion group and documentation network managed by Gary Sick under the auspices of Columbia University), February 26, 1997.

38   For the order of battle around Baghdad see Michael Eisenstadt, *Like Phoenix from the Ashes? The Future of Iraqi Military Power* (Washington, D.C.: The

Washington Institute for Near East Policy, 1993), Appendix II.

39 Even the best formations in the regular army, the 3rd *Salah al-Din,* 6th *Sa'd bin Abi Waqqas,* 10th *Nasr,* or 12th *Nu'man* armored divisions showed less professionalism than their counterparts in the Guard during the Iran–Iraq War, and in the Gulf War the gap in performance was even greater. This conclusion is derived from detailed information provided by Kenneth M. Pollack. The author is grateful for his help.

40 See *al-Thawra,* April 30, 1995.

41 See *Iraqi TV,* June 19, 1996, in *FBIS-NES-DR,* June 20, 1996, p. 38.

42 The evidence is ambiguous in several cases, but we can have a high degree of confidence that no more than ten men were executed, because the regime usually parades those who have been falsely claimed by the opposition to have been executed.

43 See, for example, *al-Sharq al-Awsat* and *al-Hayat,* quoting SAIRI, in *FBIS-NES-DR,* August 14, 1996, pp. 18–19; *Voice of Rebellious Iraq,* August 21, 1996, in *FBIS-Serial JN2108151996,* August 22, 1996; and *Voice of the People of Kurdistan,* in *FBIS-Serial NC2808180796,* August 28, 1996.

44 For details on Sha'ban, see Yunis al-Shaykh Ibrahim al-Samarra'i, *al-Qaba'il Wal Buyutat al-Hashimiyya fi al-'Iraq* (Hashemite Tribes and Houses in Iraq) (Baghdad: al-Sharq al-Jadid, 1988), p. 32.

45 See *al-Sharq al-Awsat,* July 17, 1996, quoting Iraqi sources in Amman, in *FBIS-NES-DR,* July 18, 1996, pp. 29–30; *al-Hayat,* July 12, 1996, quoting Arab sources, in *FBIS-NES-DR,* July 15, 1996, pp. 27–28.

46 Barzani had his own reasons for asking the Ba'th regime to attack Irbil. A shift in the support of some leaders of the Sorchi tribe to Talabani, as well as limited Iranian aid to Talabani, tilted the military balance in favor of Talabani's Patriotic Union of Kurdistan. To Barzani this may have seemed to be a matter of survival, but the result was that he helped tie the hands of the U.S. administration and gave Saddam what he needed, a victory that dealt a blow to U.S. intelligence operations in Kurdistan and that seemed to start rolling back the U.S.-led Operation Provide Comfort, which had helped to ensure the security of much of the Kurdish lands from the government in Baghdad.

47 See *Reuters,* September 10, 1996, in *Gulf 2000,* September 10, 1996.

48 For details about these movements, see Amatzia Baram, "Two Roads to Revolutionary Shi'ite Fundamentalism in Iraq," in Martin E. Martz and R. Scott Appleby, eds., *Accounting for Fundamentalisms: The Dymanic Character of Movements* (Chicago: University of Chicago Press and the American Academy of Arts and Sciences, 1994), pp. 531–588.

49 For the details of the agreement see *al-Mu'tamar,* November 8, 1996, p. 3.

50 See U.S. Department of State report in *Reuters,* October 17, 1997.

51 See *Reuters,* October 13 and 14, 1997; James P. Rubin, U.S. Department of State Daily Press Briefing, October 14, 1997; *Reuters World Report,* October 15, 1997; *IBC (Iraqi Broadcasting Corporation,* a London-based Iraqi opposition radio station), October 16, 1997, reporting in detail on the fighting zones, achievements, and Iraqi troop movements; *IBC,* October 17, 1997, reporting GRAD missiles, and unprecedently deep Turkish penetration, crossing the Zab river south of Aqra River to prevent PUK occupation of the Aqra Road–Hamiliton Road Junction; *Turkish Daily News,* October 17, 1997, reporting on a PUK threat to withdraw from the Ankara negotiations if Turkey does not stop straffing their positions.

52 See *Reuters World Report,* October 22, 1997.

53 Based on UN reports. See *Reuters,* October 22, 1997. See also Leon Barkho, *Reuters World Report,* October 15, 1997.

54 See Tariq 'Aziz on negotiations with both factions, Baghdad, May 11, 1998, as reported in *al-Malaff al-Iraqi* no. 78 (June 1998), p. 28. Also based on an interview with a PUK activist, May 1998.

55 For some details of the operation at the center, see Antonio Ferrari, *Corriera Della Sera,* September 11, 1996, in *FBIS-Serial BR1109101596,* September 11, 1996.

56 Telephone interview with Ambassador Robert Pelletreau, Washington, D.C., June 22, 1998.

57 See *Mideast Mirror,* October 31, 1997, quoting Kamran Karadaghi in *al-Hayat.*

58 A typical case is that of Hajj 'Abd al-Latif Mahmud Buniyya, an affluent businessman who had been one of Saddam's closest associates. In March 1994, he asked a friend of his, a captain in the Himaya, for Saddam's whereabouts, to discuss with him a very urgent business matter. The captain told him Saddam's whereabouts without having received permission to do so, and Buniyya dropped in on Saddam uninvited at his palace near Tikrit. Saddam ordered the captain to be brought to him immediately. He made Buniyya sign a huge check to the captain's family, and then had the captain executed on the spot. On his way from Baghdad to Amman later that month, Buniyya's car was attacked and he, his wife, and another person died in a hail of bullets. This information is based on two interviews with people who arrived from Baghdad and who had reliable sources there. For different versions, one involving an innocent car accident, see *Radio Monte Carlo,* April 5, 1994, in *FBIS-Serial JN0504195694,* April 5, 1994.

59 For a fairly accurate account see "Assassination Attempt Against Saddam

Reported," *Daily Telegraph,* January 18, 1994, in *FBIS-NES-DR,* January 19, 1994, pp. 40–41.

60 See, for example, an official Iraqi admission that such attacks have taken place on various occasions; *INA,* August 26, 1994, in *FBIS-Serial JN2608105794,* August 26, 1994. See also the report of a bomb, allegedly planted by a Shi'i from Basra, exploding near a hospital and wounding five, in *AFP,* September 20, 1993, in *FBIS-NES-DR,* September 24, 1993, p. 13; a rocket-propelled grenade fired at a bus full of Mujahidin e-Khalq in Baghdad, *AFP,* December 15, 1993, in *FBIS-NES-DR,* December 16, 1993, p. 27; a bomb exploding near the *al-Jumhuriyya* building, *INA,* August 23, 1994, in *FBIS-Serial JN2308202794,* August 23, 1994, p. 23.

Chapter 4

Swallowing the Bitter Pill of Resolution 986

A t 8:25 a.m. on December 10, 1996, Saddam Husayn, with great fanfare, pressed the button of Kirkuk's number one pumping station, sending the first oil to Turkey's port of Dortyol since August 1990. As reported by visitors, the masses in Baghdad celebrated in the streets by singing, chanting, and firing their guns in the air.[1] As usual in all state matters except internal security, Saddam was more concerned with the media image than with reality: The UN forced Iraq to turn off the pumps because no oil contracts had been approved yet. Still, a short while later Iraq was allowed to pump oil again.[2] In the second half of March 1997, the Iraqi people again rejoiced when the first shipments of dry food bought with the new oil revenues arrived.[3] All of this jubilation was the result of Saddam's decision to accept United Nations Security Council Resolution 986. Resolution 986 allowed Iraq limited sales of oil ($2 billion-worth every six months) to pay for food, medicine, and other humanitarian supplies. It was designed to ease the suffering of the Iraqi people while maintaining the constraint of the sanctions on Saddam.

Movement toward acceptance of Resolution 986 began in February 1996 when Saddam personally gave instructions to resume negotiations with the United Nations on the resolution. In so doing, he reversed his previous policy, which had fiercely rejected the resolution because it "infringed upon Iraq's sovereignty." From Saddam's perspective, there were two problems with the resolution. First, bringing in large amounts of food and medicine would alleviate the suffering of the Iraqi people. The misery of the average Iraqi was one of Saddam's strongest propaganda cards and one of the things he cared about least. Saddam feared that an easing of the burden of suffering for Iraq's common people would take pressure off the

UN to lift the sanctions—sanctions that affected items Saddam really did care about, like weapons and military technology purchases. Second, the resolution insisted that UN personnel supervise the sale of the oil, the purchase of supplies, and their distribution to the Iraqi people. In addition, a portion of the money would go to pay war reparations and UN expenses and another portion would be used to buy food and medicine for the Kurds, which would be distributed solely by the UN. From the UN's perspective this made perfect sense: Saddam's previous track record left few with the impression he could be trusted to feed his own people and not horde the money for his loyalists. From Saddam's perspective, however, UN oversight was a terrible affront to his dignity and his role as the final arbiter of all activity in Iraq.

Saddam's eventual accpetance of Resolution 986 came only at the end of a long series of events that radically altered the context of Baghdad's decision making. Some of these events were deleterious for Iraq and helped convince Saddam that he had no choice but to accept the deal. Others were positive for Iraq—or really, for Saddam—and convinced him that he could afford to go ahead and swallow an unpalatable resolution without a risk to his reputation in the eyes of his power base. The defection of Husayn Kamil weakened Saddam, but his return to Iraq and his murder contributed to the deference Saddam received from his power base. The revelation of the coup plot in the Republican Guard in the summer of 1996 strengthened Saddam's short-term deterrence vis-à-vis his army and Guard officers, but it also sent a message that the Guard's long-term loyalty was in jeopardy. Saddam's offensive against Irbil reinvigorated his image as a bold strategist and allowed him to retreat on another front, that of national pride, and accept Resolution 986. Yet, by far the most important (and negative) factor shaping Saddam's decision to accept Resolution 986 was the crisis in the Iraqi economy that first erupted in December 1995 and worsened in January 1996 creating severe inflationary spirals that threatened to tear apart the entire country.

Inflation, Political Stability, and Oil Sales

Saddam Husayn's greatest political asset is probably his ability to cow the Iraqi people into submission. Students of Iraqi history were astounded to see how quickly and effectively the Ba'th regime managed to pacify a nation that had been known for its volatility. The metamorphosis derived from the ability of the Ba'th to employ both *al-tarhib* (tremendous terror) against any real or perceived opposition, and *al-targhib* (considerable enticement) to encourage quiesence. For the general public, enticement meant a higher standard of living, financed by the oil boom of the mid-1970s, and political stability. The latter came at a very high price: Any political opposition usually resulted in arrest, torture, and death, often extending to the accused's family as well. But the Ba'th regime created a system that guaranteed an acceptable standard of living, protection from unauthorized crime, and a reasonably functional—albeit heavily corrupt—bureaucracy, for those who were ready to avoid politics and overlook the leadership's transgressions.

Even under the sanctions regime, some of the old targhib still endures. Until March–April 1997, when the first food deliveries permitted by Resolution 986 arrived in Iraq, the population had received fifteen days' worth of dry food staples every month, practically free of charge. Free dry staple foods for two weeks out of every month is not something to be dismissed lightly. Dependence on these staples is total, and consequently, Iraqis tend to see any disruption of the political system as a threat to their own livelihood.

Yet, Saddam's insistence on maintaining the public's passivity by disbursing grain and rice to his people created another problem for the regime. To finance the purchase of this food, as well as to provide for his loyalists and internal security personnel, Saddam found it necessary to print increasing quantities of money. Iraq's hard currency reserves, coupled with the small amounts Iraq is able to raise through smuggling, were able to cover much of these expenses for several years. This kept inflation under control during the first years of the embargo. Between January 1993 and January 1996 the annual inflation rate, as measured by the dinar–dollar exchange rate, went up but still remained at around 330 percent. This is obviously quite high by most standards, but under the circumstances was no small achievement, because it enabled the economy to continue to function. Yet, Iraq's reserves began to dwindle to such an extent that Baghdad increasingly had to resort to the printing press. As a result, beginning in 1994, inflation began to creep ever higher in Iraq, putting ever greater pressure on average Iraqis—who had to buy their food and other necessities in the market for the other two weeks of every month not covered by Saddam's largesse. Soldiers, bureaucrats, teachers, and others who were entirely dependent on government salaries were particularly hard hit: Their salaries generally did not keep pace with inflation because the state could not afford to link the salaries of the cumbersome bureaucracy to the index, and these individuals had few skills they could use to barter for food or other goods.

As early as the second half of 1993, a pattern began to emerge that caused Saddam great concern. In late 1993, in the face of a sudden price hike, 'Udayy's *Babil* began complaining that government factories were making illegal profits and brazenly suggested that profiteering private merchants should be executed, "as happens in capitalistic America itself."[4] In March 1994, in response to rumors that Iraq was about to see the sanctions lifted by the UN, the value of the Iraqi dinar stabilized. But when the Security Council voted not to lift the embargo the dinar plunged, losing almost 20 percent of its value against the U.S. dollar between April and May 1994, and then losing another 55 percent between May and June, according to an official (and very conservative) Iraqi source.[5] When it needed dollars, the Ministry of Finance would often buy them on the local market, thus pushing the price higher. In particular, whenever there was a rumor that sanctions were about to end, the value of the dinar tended to rise briefly, allowing government officials to buy large amounts of (relatively) cheap dollars. This way the government and some individuals, mostly Saddam's family members, profited while the inflationary trend continued unabated.

In May 1994, Saddam recognized he had to deal with the inflationary pressure before it seriously undermined the Iraqi economy, and thus his rule. He took over the premiership and enacted draconian punishments against profiteers, thieves, and corrupt officials while simultaneously releasing various commodities onto the market at reduced prices. The result was a resounding, but short-lived, success. Over the next three months, the dinar–dollar rate remained virtually unchanged. Yet, in September the dinar started a new nose-dive. On September 25, the Ministry of Trade announced that most food rations would be cut by 33 percent to 50 percent as a "temporary measure." In addition, the number of those eligible to receive rations was restricted to 3.5 million families of employees (as opposed to those who were self-employed). Although government employees received an ID 2,000 raise per month, the regime did not try to hide the fact that the cuts would hurt.[6] Nonetheless, at the end of September 1994 Saddam promised his people, "Prosperity is on the way! Prosperity is on the way!"[7]

Yet within a few days, it was not inflation that was heading south, but Iraqi tanks. At the start of October, Saddam ordered the Republican Guard south, to the Kuwaiti border.[8] It is far from clear whether Saddam actually intended to re-invade Kuwait in October 1994.[9] He may have intended to attack Kuwait to try to force the international community to lift or ease the sanctions and thereby alleviate his economic crisis. Alternatively, he may have intended only to threaten Kuwait to create a war-scare that would distract the Iraqi people and prevent a mass-protest over the ration cuts. Whatever the truth, people in Baghdad were petrified, and the cuts paled in significance. Although this gambit succeeded in finding Saddam a short-term solution to his economic problems, the result of Saddam's aggressiveness was that the UN Security Council imposed new regulations on Iraq. Resolution 949 forbade Baghdad from moving any additional forces (that is, the Republican Guard) into southern Iraq, thereby making it more difficult for Saddam to resort to this measure in the future.[10]

As could be expected, the breathing space Saddam had bought himself with his threatened attack on Kuwait did not last. In 1995, the same inflationary pattern repeated itself. Between February and March of that year the dinar lost 36 percent of its value. After several false starts in which Iraqi deputy prime minister Tariq Aziz seemed to accept the resolution and then quickly backtracked, the Security Council adopted Resolution 986 on April 14 without Iraqi acceptance.[11] This was the first resolution to allow large-scale Iraqi oil sales since the invasion of Kuwait in August 1990.

The specific terms of the resolution allowed all states to import Iraqi petroleum sufficient to produce no more than US$1 billion in revenue every ninety days. Subject to arrangements that would prevent misuse of the funds, Iraq was then empowered to use the proceeds of these oil sales to purchase foodstuffs, medicine, and certain equipment necessary for the well-being of the Iraqi populace. Moreover, roughly 13 percent of the proceeds of the oil sales (between $130 million and $150 million every ninety days) would be provided to the UN Inter-Agency Humanitarian Program, operating in Iraqi Kurdistan, to purchase food, medicine and other humanitarian supplies for Iraq's Kurdish population. Another 30 percent would be earmarked for a compensation fund to pay reparations to the victims (mainly Kuwaitis) of Iraq's aggression in 1990. Other sums would be earmarked to meet the costs of UN activities in Iraq. Altogether, the central government of Iraq would receive about 53 percent of the total revenues.[12]

When it was first announced, Iraq's National Assembly and the Revolutionary Command Council (its nominal parliament and "politburo," respectively) rejected the resolution ferociously, and the regime organized mass demonstrations against it. The government dismissed the resolution on the grounds that it infringed upon Iraq's sovereignty, and so besmirched its national honor.[13] This argument was perfectly true, but since March 1991 Iraq had already agreed to so many humiliating limitations imposed on its sovereignty that such intransigence seemed bizarre to many observers, but not to Saddam. He had to take into account the frustrations of his senior party and internal security officials, the army, and the Republican Guard. In the Ba'thi political culture, it is far safer to look unnecessarily intransigent than weak. Only when all other options have been clearly exhausted, and when Saddam has demonstrated beyond a shadow of doubt that he is tougher than anyone else, will he risk making concessions. Resolution 986 did not meet these conditions in April 1995. Following his army's defeat to the Kurds and the INC, Saddam apparently feared that a sudden rush to embrace the resolution would make him look weak, dependent on the UN (and the United States), and unable to solve Iraq's problems.

The result of Iraq's stubbornness was predictable. Within weeks, the dinar suddenly went into a free fall again: Between May and June 1995 it lost roughly 47 percent of its value, in July and August, another 4 percent; by September another 19 percent, and by October still another 15 percent.[14] This inflationary upsurge forced Saddam Husayn to take drastic measures. On December 2, Saddam stopped the Iraqi government from printing new money,[15] imposing new taxes and surcharges, and permitting salary increases, while he simultaneously authorized a "revision" (that is, reduction) of government subsidies, an increase in the price of government services, and the sale of government cars, spares, and other goods. Finally, Saddam decreed that food and other commodities be sold 10 percent below market value.[16] The Iraqi public, however, had largely lost faith in the regime's ability to redeem the situation without massive oil sales. The exchange rate continued to deteriorate, albeit at a slower pace. In November 1995 the value of the dinar had been 2,556 to the dollar, but during the first half of January 1996 it reached nearly 3,000 to the dollar.[17] In response to the dinar's fall, food prices went up steeply, increasing popular discontent.[18]

The very real threat of an uncontrollable inflation forced Saddam to accept the ultimate medicine. On January 16, Deputy Prime Minister Tariq 'Aziz requested UN secretary general Boutros Boutros-Ghali to invite Iraq to renegotiate Resolution 986.[19] Moreover, his old allies in Paris and Moscow sweetened the deal for Saddam. The French and Russians promised him that "in exchange" for Iraq's acceptance of 986 they would push hard for the total lifting of UN sanctions.[20] This greatly eased Saddam's fear that the application of 986 would alleviate the suffering of Iraq's populace to such an extent that it would dissipate the humanitarian pressure on the Security Council to lift the sanctions.

On January 20, Iraqi radio announced that Baghdad had accepted the UN invitation.[21] This proclamation was greeted by jubilation in Baghdad.[22] Between January 16 and February 7, the value of the dinar skyrocketed from almost 3,000 per dollar to roughly 400 per dollar.[23]

The question remains as to whether Iraq was so economically strapped that it had no other choice but to accept Resolution 986. As long as Saddam refused to give up his remaining nonconventional weapons and thereby satisfy the terms of Resolution 687, which prevented Iraq from selling oil, Baghdad had to find other means of stabilizing the dinar. But, in theory, Saddam could have accomplished this same goal by pumping dollars and inexpensive food into the Iraqi market. When he accepted 986, it is quite possible that Saddam still had several billion dollars stashed in his vaults that could have been used for this purpose. But Saddam usually thinks in the long term. Had he continued to reject 986, he would have had to spend ever growing sums of his dwindling foreign currency reserves on subsidies to avert economic chaos. The seasonal collapse of the dinar and corresponding price hikes in 1994 and 1995 convinced him of this. Yet, Saddam was not about to squander the last of his financial reserves. When Iraq's national honor had to be balanced against his own cash reserves, the cash won out.

Nevertheless, even then Saddam was not yet immediately ready to accept the oil-for-food deal. After further haggling, another agreement was reached on May 20, 1996. In working out the administrative details of this agreement, however, Iraq again brought the negotiations to a standstill.[24] Despite strenuous efforts by the UN negotiators to persuade Iraq to proceed with implementation, Baghdad dug in its heels on several technical issues. So frustrating had the process become that many began to speculate that Saddam had not changed his mind and was simply proclaiming his acceptance of the resolution to restore confidence in the dinar but he had no intent actually to proceed with the deal. Indeed, observers even opined that Saddam's assault on Irbil that August was evidence that Saddam did not really want the oil agreement and was actively looking for ways to sabotage it.

In fact, nothing could have been more erroneous. Saddam's attack on Irbil was a crucial aspect of his acceptance of Resolution 986. The Iraqi president needed a military victory that would boost his masculine image in the eyes of his power base—the Republican Guard, the tribes, the security apparati, the party—before he could capitulate politically. Taking Irbil ended the humiliation that began some eighteen months earlier with the Kurdish offensive near Irbil. This provided Saddam with a near-perfect alibi. He was able to cross the psychological hurdle of accepting the humiliating terms of 986 only when he had given the Guard a new military triumph and hammered home his own reputation as ruthless, strong, and in complete control of Iraq. Thus, far from sabotaging the oil-for-food deal, Baghdad's attack on Irbil was what made it possible.

At long last, on the afternoon of November 25, 1996, the Iraqi News Agency announced: "Iraq has informed the UN that it is ready to implement immediately the Memorandum of Understanding . . . [of] May 20th . . . of oil-for-food." Part of the senior Iraqi leadership and the media were taken by complete surprise by the sudden decision.[25] But for the Iraqi public, all that mattered was that food and other commodity prices dropped steeply immediately after the announcement.[26]

THE PROS AND CONS OF 986 FOR SADDAM

The advantages accruing to the Ba'th regime from accepting Resolution 986 have been considerable. First, the sale of oil has greatly improved Iraq's international and regional standing. Many states have shown an interest in doing business with Iraq and have been ready to pay with diplomatic assets to get their foot in the door. Second, the food and medicines being distributed to the population have alleviated the suffering of the people. This does not imply a return to pre-1990 standards for health and nutrition: Until the invasion of Kuwait, Iraq spent no less than $2 billion annually and possibly closer to $3 billion for food imports alone,[27] while the resolution as currently configured will leave Iraq only about $2.4 billion for both food and medicines—and for a population that has grown from 20 million to 22 million since the Gulf War, (Iraqi reports of an epidemic of infant mortality notwithstanding). Even this problem may soon evaporate, as the Security Council recently tabled a new resolution that would greatly expand the amount of oil Iraq is allowed to sell under Resolution 986. Even if Iraq is unable to spend as much on food and medicine as it did before the invasion of Kuwait, the Iraqi people will still feel a substantial improvement all the same. Finally, from Saddam's perspective, the main positive aspect of the deal is that the revenues that will accrue from the new oil sales will save Iraq close to $1 billion annually— money the regime had been spending on food imports and that now can be used to upgrade the perks of the inner circle, reinvigorate the Republican Guard, and finance the smuggling of weapons technology.

So far, the disadvantages of the deal for the regime have turned out to be minor. The Iraqi people understand that the UN, rather than their own government, is supervising the entire process. But at the grass-roots level, the public sees only the old system: The food is distributed by 53,000 neighborhood grocery stores and the presence of the 150 foreign supervisors is very limited. The medicine bought under the deal will be dispensed through government hospitals and pharmacies, and consequently here too ordinary Iraqis will not feel the UN presence.[28] Thus, the people will continue to see Saddam as the source of their livelihood. As for the humiliation to the regime inherent in accepting the resolution, it is of no political significance. In the eyes of Saddam's power base it has been dwarfed by his exploits in Kurdistan and the man in the street is so relieved to know that his food rations are improving that any affront to Iraq's dignity will gladly be overlooked. Indeed, the most important downside for Saddam is that the international humanitarian pressure to lift the embargo may subside now that the UN has created a mechanism to ease the suffering of the Iraqi people. But with his well-oiled propaganda machine he stands a good chance to cash in on the remaining suffering: There is no doubt in large and especially Shi'i areas that much suffering will remain for a while at least.

Still, Saddam's decision to provoke a crisis with the UN in October–November 1997 was probably driven, at least in part, by the fear that, soon after the acceptance of Resolution 986, the humanitarian issue will no longer be relevant and the embargo will stay. Saddam's major foreign policy acts are usually motivated by a combination of perceived opportunities and threats. Thus the invasion of Iran was prompted by both a perception that the Islamic revolution had greatly weakened Iran's armed forces, and a fear that Khomeini's charisma and message could spark a similar revolt within Iraq if he were not overthrown. Similarly, Saddam attacked Kuwait because Iran's defeat and the decline of the USSR and what looked like U.S. passivity created a power vacuum in the Gulf. Concomitantly, Iraq's own economic problems created a need for additional wealth—which

Kuwait had in abundance. It is certainly true that, during the summer of 1997, Saddam perceived the feckless behavior of France and Russia and the ever-weaker responses of the Security Council to his provocations as a window of opportunity for him to further divide the international community and have sanctions eased or lifted. Nevertheless, it is also likely that Saddam ignited the crisis and then kept it burning no matter how hard the international community tried to douse it, to remind the international community that he will not allow the embargo to be forgotten. Full cooperation with the United Nations Special Commision on Iraq (UNSCOM) as a way to lift the embargo, however, is out of the question: At least as demonstrated by his *modus operandi*, as he sees it, an embargo is less dangerous for him than the voluntary disclosure of all his remaining technological secrets. It is quite clear that ultimately, he intends both to keep key elements of his WMD program and to get the embargo lifted.

SADDAM AND UNSCOM

Soon after the first deliveries of food, Saddam demonstrated his fear that alleviating the suffering of the Iraqi people would undermine his case to have the sanctions lifted. The first contract with the UN under Resolution 986 ended on June 8, 1997. At that time, Iraq stopped its oil exports, demanded more freedom in signing oil contracts, and accused the United States of deliberate rigidity and sluggishness in implementing the resolution. Iraq refused to resume exporting oil through the Turkish pipeline for two months, and ended up with only 24 days (rather than three months) to export $1 billion worth of oil. In the meantime, the regime announced another reduction in food rations (by some 30 percent) in September 1997, which it then blamed on supposed U.S. obstructiveness.[29] Clearly the technicalities Baghdad was complaining about were meaningless to the Iraqi people, and the regime was simply using them as an excuse to drag out the suffering of its people and blame it on the United States. Yet, such a drastic and unexpected decrease in Iraqi rations, especially so soon after the euphoria of the first food deliveries, could have created dangerous discontent at home. Thus, as he did in October 1994, this seems to be another reason behind the major crisis with the UN and the United States: namely, to try to disract Iraqis from the real source of their misery.

Since the inception of the UNSCOM inspection regime in 1991, Saddam has tried to obstruct its activities by any means possible. He has tried to control the composition of the teams. He has tried to set limits on where they could go and when they could go there. He has hidden information and weapons. He has refused to allow UN officials access to sites suspected of hiding material related to his weapons of mass destruction (WMD) programs. He has smuggled spare parts and technology into Iraq. His mukhabarat have harassed UN personnel in outrageous fashion, to the extent of threatening to poison then–UNSCOM chairman Rolf Ekeus. He has lied, fabricated, and obfuscated in every single report to UNSCOM. When caught in these lies, Baghdad's explanations have been unusual to say the least. For instance, as reported by an UNSCOM official, after Iraq disconnected the cameras monitoring many of its former WMD production facilities in October 1997, the Iraqis claimed that the wires had been cut by a "wandering psychopath" who for some reason worked in the Iraqi WMD sites, forgot to take his medicine, went berserk, and severed the camera's wires at each facility, but did not touch anything in the facility except the cameras. The Iraqi authorities warned UNSCOM that the same psychopath might forget to take his medicine again.

Of course, there was a period of learning for the Iraqis in which they committed several blunders, but over time they have become increasingly skillful in deceiving the inspectors. In early January 1993, the Security Council declared Iraq in "an unacceptable and material breach" of its resolutions because of Iraq's uncooperative behavior. This language became synonymous with authorization for Gulf War coalition members to employ military force against Iraq, and in mid-January the United States struck Iraq with cruise missiles. On June 10, 1993 Iraq prevented UNSCOM teams from installing cameras in a former missile factory. The Security Council again declared Iraq in "material and unacceptable breach" of the cease-fire and Iraq, having learned its lesson, quickly reversed itself and allowed UNSCOM to install the cameras. Since then, Saddam has tried to be careful to obstruct the teams' work in a way that would spare him U.S. military reprisals. In this he has been aided mainly by the French and Russian delegations to the Security Council. Although in principle both Moscow and Paris are committed to the dismantling of Iraq's weapons of mass destruction, in practice these two permanent members of the Security Council have made it progressively more difficult to impose the UN's will on Iraq on this matter. The result is that Iraq has gotten away with very serious obstructions that, in all probability, have enabled it to prevent important components of its WMD programs from falling into UNSCOM's hands.

There have been, however, a few strange exceptions to Saddam's rule of avoiding an all-out clash. One such exceptional case was the October 1994 crisis, when Iraq announced that it would no longer cooperate with the UN and massed the Republican Guard on the Kuwaiti border. Eventually, when threatened with military reprisals, Saddam pulled back his troops and returned to his low-profile obstructions. It is entirely possible that Saddam did intend to attack Kuwait again, but even if he did not, this incident was very unusual: His opting for a high-risk, high-profile operation could have ended in a preventive U.S. attack on his Republican Guards. In May–July 1995, Saddam began to hatch another high-profile confrontation. On July 17, in his Revolution Day speech, Saddam declared that Iraq would cease to cooperate with the UN unless the embargo were lifted by August 31.[30] Earlier, senior Iraqis warned Ambassador Ekeus that Iraq would tie UNSCOM officials to machines in the installations that would be the prime targets for U.S. air raids. What was so perplexing about this case was that at that moment UNSCOM had been ready to move closer to giving Iraq a clean bill of health on its chemical warfare and ballistic missile programs, in exchange for information regarding its biological weapons, which would have been a huge step for Iraq.[31] The defection of Husayn Kamil in August 1995 aborted the Iraqi confrontation plan, sending the regime into a panic and prompting it to reveal huge amounts of material on its WMD programs that it had previously concealed. Most important were details on Iraq's biological warfare program. This convinced Ekeus and UNSCOM that Iraq was far from complying with any aspect of the resolutions. Had Husayn Kamil not defected that August, it is very likely that the confrontation of October–November 1997 would have occured in 1995. Indeed, in 1997, Iraqi vice president Taha Yasin Ramadan disclosed that in the summer of 1995, Saddam had intended to initiate a crisis and force the UN to lift the sanctions, but he had to abort his plans when Husayn Kamil defected. Saddam shelved the idea and was able to set it in motion again only in the autumn of 1997.[32]

These instances where Saddam crossed the line and nearly provoked a harsh response from the Security Council or the United States had an accumulated impact. They eroded the will of the Security Council and its responses to Iraqi provocations gradually weakened. In 1996, despite constant Iraqi obstructions, only once did the Security Council accept a U.S.–British proposal to use language that could have legitimized military action. On June 14, 1996, after particularly severe obstructions, the Security Council armed Ekeus with a strong statement,[33] and the Iraqis took him more seriously and agreed to a joint document, outlining future procedures for surprise UNSCOM inspections, which both sides signed in Baghdad on June 22.[34] Yet, less than a month after the agreement was signed, on July 16—and again in mid-August—UN inspectors were blocked from entering suspected Iraqi WMD sites.[35] The weak response of the Security Council convinced Baghdad in late November to deny UNSCOM officials permission to export 130 missile engines they wanted to study. Only in February 1997, after another strong UN warning, would Iraq relent.[36]

In 1997, this pattern continued. In June, Iraq confronted UNSCOM and even endangered the life of one team member during a helicopter flight. The United States and Britain demanded strong measures, although only of a diplomatic nature: a ban on travel by all Iraqi officials involved in the military–industrial complex—including Tariq Aziz—and an indefinite suspension of the sixty-day sanction review until Iraq cooperated again. France and Russia led a coalition that objected to the travel ban. It required impromptu negotiations between Presidents Bill Clinton and Boris Yeltsin themselves to resolve the issue: Iraq was given a warning and the Security Council would refrain from making a decision about the travel ban until October when UNSCOM would again report on Iraqi noncompliance.[37] This was an important victory for Iraq, and it seems to have enhanced Saddam's confidence that he was almost immune to UN reprisals.

On October 6, 1997, Ambassador Richard Butler, the new chief of UNSCOM, presented his report to the Security Council. Although it had made progress on removing ballistic missiles and chemical weapons, he reported, Iraq had failed to give "a remotely credible account" of its biological weapons industry. Worse still, as Butler reported, between June and October 1997, "the commission has encountered a pattern of Iraqi blockages and evidence of removal and/or destruction of documents and material at sensitive sites under inspection. Iraq denied any biological weapons' planning, but UNSCOM has ample proof that such a program was underway. Likewise, Iraq failed to produce information in regard to the most potent chemical nerve agent, VX. Most serious were two cases in which Tariq Aziz personally obstructed the supervisors' work."[38] The International Atomic Energy Agency similarly pointed out that it still needed to continue the investigation of Iraq's nuclear program because documents were missing and the information Baghdad had provided had significant gaps.[39]

Despite UNSCOM's highly critical report and its prior threats, the Security Council again refused to take firm action against Iraq. The United States and Britain first tried to have the Council make good on its warning from June and impose the limited travel ban, but it could not get the Security Council to agree. Then, Washington and London proposed a measure that would impose the new sanctions automatically if, by April 1998, Iraq was still not fully cooperating with UNSCOM. Yet, a coalition of the French, Russians, Chinese, Kenyans, and Egyptians prevented even this. Eventually, on October 23, 1997, the Security Council adopted Resolution 1134, expressing its "firm intention" to restrict the travel of Iraqi officials if, by April 1998, Iraq did not meet its obligations. Even this was not a unanimous vote: France, Russia, China, Kenya, and Egypt all abstained.[40]

Baghdad watched these events very carefully and saw them as clear signs of a serious rift within the Security Council. Saddam saw his chance and he took it. On October 27, the Iraqi parliament recommended to Saddam and the Revolutionary Command Council (RCC) that Iraq cease all cooperation with UNSCOM until a clear and short timetable for the lifting of the embargo was established.[41] Such a recommendation could have been made only on Saddam's orders. The next day, the RCC issued a resolution barring all Americans from entering Iraq as part of the inspection teams, because they were all spies. The Security Council held an urgent meeting and, finally, all fifteen members agreed on a statement condemning Iraq and warning of the "serious consequences of Iraq's failure to comply immediately and fully with its obligations under the relevant resolutions."[42] Nevertheless, Iraq ordered all ten Americans then in Iraq to leave within one week. Three others who later landed at Habbaniyya airfield were sent back to Bahrain.

From there, Saddam continued to push the crisis forward. The October debate in the Security Council and the abstention of the five "coalition" members—even after the United States and Britain had watered down their proposal—apparently had convinced Saddam to try to split the Security Council further. The Security Council's statement warning of serious consequences, probably was a surprise to Saddam, suggesting a minimal level of solidarity that he had not expected. Yet, even when he realized that rather than splitting the Security Council he had actually managed to unite it, he continued his confrontational posture and even escalated the crisis, threatening to shoot down American U2 surveillance airplanes flying photographic reconnaissance missions on behalf of UNSCOM. Moreover, he ordered the beginning of the dismantling of the surveillance equipment UNSCOM had installed to monitor Iraq's former WMD factories.

This risky approach was a clear depature from Iraq's more common-place pattern of obstructions. Usually, Saddam had been content to ham-string the UNSCOM teams on specific occasions when they were getting close to a location where arms, parts, or documents were hidden. In those instances, the Iraqis would routinely obstruct the UNSCOM teams however they could for several hours—or occasionally even days—to give *al-Amn al-Khass* (the Special Security Organization [SSO]) the incriminating evidence. Occasionally, however, Saddam would challenge the entire inspection regime, and even the UN's right to continue to sanction Iraq until Baghdad complied with its obligations to the satisfaction of the Security Council. As in October 1995, and, less directly, August–September 1996, Iraq was now seeking a high-profile confrontation that would gain it media attention, but that also involved a much higher risk of military confrontation.

This sudden escalation of Saddam's strategy suggests that other forces were at work in addition to his desire to exploit the opportunity created by France and Russia's defection from the international coalition. In the first place, Saddam has told his people almost every day since 1991 that Iraq won the Gulf War because his regime remains in power and remains defiant; he therefore needed to demonstrate his defiance occasionally. Second, Saddam cannot allow the international community to forget how desperately he wants the sanctions lifted, especially since Baghdad's acceptance of Resolution 986. Third, it was important for Saddam to demonstrate to the long-suffering Iraqi people—who have repeatedly been promised a quick end to sanctions—that their leader is doing his best to keep his promise. Yet, the timing of the crisis suggests that even more pressing internal political considerations may also have played a role.

In the past, Saddam's riskiest moves against the UN and the United States have been provoked by domestic problems that threatened to undermine Saddam's support among his power base. In October 1994 Saddam suspended all cooperation with UNSCOM and threatened to invade Kuwait when the free-fall of the dinar forced him to take extremely painful measures (slashing the free food staples) that could have turned the Iraqi people, and many of his supporters, against him. Likewise, Saddam's still-born crisis in the summer of 1995 was prompted by a drastic decline in the value of the dinar. Also, by June–July 1995 it became clear that UNSCOM was adamant on investigating Iraq's biological weapons, a new area that

Iraq had hoped it could keep secret. This diminished the importance of the "clean bill of health" over missiles and chemical weapons and meant that the embargo was there to stay. This, in turn, called for drastic action. The brewing crisis of June, July, and August 1995 ended only when the defection of Husayn Kamil that August threw the government into a panic. Even the summer 1996 crisis with UNSCOM over inspection sites appears to have been provoked, at least in part, by internal politics. At the same time, Saddam had purged numerous officers in the Special Republican Guard after the revelation of the coup attempt in conjunction with the Republican Guard planned for August 1996. Saddam needed to refocus the Guard's and the SSO's ire on UNSCOM and demonstrate to them that he would not allow UNSCOM to deprive Iraq of the powerful (and prestigious) weapons of mass destruction Saddam had entrusted to them.

According to an interview with UN officials,[43] the October–November 1997 crisis started with an impasse between Iraqi security forces and an UNSCOM team. Past record suggests that an important longer-term reason for the autumn 1997 confrontation may have been to shore up his standing among his power base: the army officers, internal security establishment, and tribes that support him. That many in the general population—in particular city folk—are bankrupt, and suffering is far less important to Saddam than what the Iraqi security establishment thinks. And, to the extent that one can judge based on a small sample of interviews, many in this establishment are incensed at the destruction of their weapons of mass destruction. It is their duty to guard Iraqi national security against two formidable neighbors: Iran and Turkey. An armed conflict with either cannot be counted out, and the members of Iraq's establishment feel that WMDs may be the equalizer they need. Israel, too, is a potential enemy with tremendous military capabilities.

No less important, the Iraqi political and military establishments have been indoctrinated by the Ba'th regime to look on Iraq as the leader of the Arabs and their defender against Iran, Israel, and Western "imperialism." Nowhere is this role better presented than in the Ba'thi–Iraqi national anthem, which proclaims, "Our almighty [Iraqi] people (sha'b) is splendor and eruption/We are citadels of strength built by our comrades/You will always be the Arabs' savior O Iraq!/ As bright suns make our morning from the dark!"[44] This theme, Iraq as leader of the Arab struggle and Arab unity, figures prominently in Saddam's public speeches. Iraq's nonconventional weapons are an indispensable tool in this context, particularly now that Iraq has lost so much of its conventional force. Saddam may feel an overriding need to convince his followers that he can defend the most important components of Iraq's nonconventional weaponry tenaciously and successfully.[45] He seems to be afraid that total surrender to UNSCOM will cast him in a bad light in the eyes of his security establishment. Saddam fears that he will be seen as a weak leader who has lost his *sharaf* (manly honor). Whenever he discusses the traits he values, this particular one ranks very high.

Finally, as a result of the Ba'th way of thinking, Saddam feels his regime is vulnerable to an onslaught by his country's Shi'i majority or by foreign powers—Iran or the United States, and less so Israel or Turkey—and this sense of vulnerability provides him with a powerful incentive to retain the most potent components of his WMD program. This belief was enhanced when Iran threatened Basra between 1982 and 1987, when the allied forces advanced north of Kuwait and within reach of Baghdad in 1991, and when the Shi'i and Kurdish revolts rocked the foundations of the regime in the same year. Since it took power in 1968, the Ba'th regime has been trying to create the impression inside Iraq that if it goes down, it will take with it much of Iraq; since 1991 it has been trying to impress that view outside Iraq as well. As a result of a deliberate scare campaign on the part of the regime, there is now a widespread belief among Iraqis that Saddam will not leave power without inflicting a devastating blow on his own country. Similarly, Iraqi officers interrogated by UNSCOM workers in Baghdad reported that Saddam has ordered SSO commanders of nonconventional missile batteries to fire their missiles if communications with Baghdad are severed either as a result of a nuclear attack or if Baghdad is being attacked by the allied forces' ground troops. In other words, Saddam and his SSO loyalists see the nonconventional arsenal as a powerful deterrent against any attempt to end their rule. That they would give up those weapons, then, seems highly unlikely.[46]

Although it would be surprising if a domestic motive behind Saddam's actions did not exist, his behavior cannot be explained solely by his need to demonstrate defiance. In October 1994 and again in November 1997, Saddam's courses of action were more risky than would have been necessary for propaganda purposes. Clearly, he is not acting defiant just for the record: He is taking precipitous action to prevent the destruction of his weapons and to erode the will of the Security Council to continue the embargo. This too is a high-priority goal, because he must alleviate his ruling elites' fear that the embargo regime will stay on as long as Saddam is in power. To keep his WMDs, Saddam seems ready to pay the price in terms of further delays in the Security Council decision to lift the embargo. Indeed, by obstructing UNSCOM's work he has delayed the lifting of the embargo for seven years and counting, sacrificing roughly $120 billion in oil revenues in the process. But he cannot afford to delay the lifting of the embargo for much longer. In short, it is clear that Saddam is determined to retain his WMD arsenal and that he is ready to pay a very high price to keep it. Of course, he is aware of the unstated but widely understood American–British position that no matter what UNSCOM reports to the Security Council, sanctions will remain in place as long as he remains president of Iraq.[47] From his perspective, if the United States and Britain can impose their will on the Security Council indefinitely, then regardless of UNSCOM's reports he will not see an end to sanctions. In this case, he would have nothing to lose: Even if he were to disclose all of his technological secrets, the Americans and the British would still keep the embargo on his regime forever. Yet, Saddam also has to consider the possibility that a clean bill of health from UNSCOM will allow Iraq's friends in the UN—France, Russia, China, some of the Arab countries, and a few others—to erode the determination of London and Washington to keep the embargo in place. Indeed, the official Arab position as expressed in both the Arab league and the GCC has been that if Iraq is given a clean bill of health from UNSCOM and meets its commitments to Kuwait, it will be brought back into the Arab fold. Should this occur, the United States and Great Britain would find it very difficult to veto a motion to lift the sanctions on Iraq.

Furthermore, Saddam may see a change in U.S. policy toward Iraq, as suggested by President Clinton himself in an interview with Jim Lehrer:

> If [Saddam] cares [about his people] he would open all these [weapons] sites . . . If he is telling the truth, and there is really nothing there . . . [then] what benefit does the U.S. have now for stopping the UN from lifting he sanctions. . . . Even though we have got reservations about it, we would have a hard time answering that question.[48]

In other words, Saddam should have recognized by now that if Iraq were to cooperate fully with UNSCOM, within a few months his chances of seeing the end of the embargo would be excellent. Yet he refuses to comply. Clearly, retaining his WMDs takes precedence for him over having the embargo lifted. But lifting the embargo is still of tremendous importance to him. If his power base feels that he is unable to deliver both goals—retaining Iraq's WMDs and ending the embargo—he will gradually lose their support. Thus his high-profile crises are designed to break the diplomatic ice that has locked in the embargo. Iraq has enjoyed some success in this effort. In November 1997, Russia was able to focus UN Security Council discussions on issues like the composition of UNCSOM's supervising teams, U2 overflights, and, generally speaking, UNSCOM's impartiality and fairness, rather than Iraqi compliance—or the lack thereof.

NOTES

1 See *Reuters*, December 10, 1996.

2 See President Bill Clinton's letter to the Speaker of the House of Representatives and the President Pro Tempore of the Senate, *U.S. Newswire,* January 8, 1997.

3 Based on reports of news agencies, as quoted in *Ha'aretz,* March 24, 1997.

4 Mazhar 'Arif, *Babil,* November 6, 1993, in *Foreign Broadcast Information Service–Near East and South Asia–Daily Report (FBIS-NES-DR),* January 13, 1994, p. 5.

5 Computed by the author from a report by the Iraqi Central Bank, published in *Iraq TV Network,* February 9, 1996, in *FBIS-NES-DR,* February 13, 1996, pp. 30–32.

6 Based on *INA,* September 25, 1994, in *FBIS-Serial JN2509132994,* September 25, 1994; reports of the news agencies as quoted in *al-Malaff al-'Iraqi,* no. 34 (October 1994), p. 36; Saddam to the command of the Baghdad party branch, *Babil,* September 28, 1994.

7 Saddam to the command of the Baghdad party branch, *Babil,* September 28, 1994.

8 See *al-Thawra,* October 9, 1994.

9 After his defection, Husayn Kamil argued categorically that Saddam did intend to invade Kuwait to try to force the UN to repeal the sanctions, but Saddam was deterred from doing so by the rapid response of the United States and the speedy build-up of U.S. military forces in the Persian Gulf. Although Husayn Kamil certainly had an incentive to paint Saddam in the most lurid tones possible, he was not known to have lied in any of his debriefings. See "Husayn Kamil on Army Strength, Saddam Fedayeen," *al-Watan al-'Arabi,* in *FBIS-NES,* November 27, 1995, p. 33.

10 President Clinton's letter, *U.S. Newswire,* January 8, 1997.

11 See *INA,* April 7 and 8, 1995, in *FBIS-NES-DR,* April 10, 1995, pp. 33–34. UN Security Council, *Resolution 986 (1995) Adopted by the Security Council at its 3519th Meeting on 14 April 1995.*

12 UN Security Council, *Interim Report of the Secretary General on the Implementation of Security Council Resolution 986 (1995),* New York, November 25, 1996, p. 9.

13 See, for example, Foreign Minister Muhammad Sa'id al-Sahhaf to *al-Hayat,* May 20, 1995, in *FBIS-NES-DR,* May 24, 1995, p. 26. The separate treatment of Kurdistan was the main danger the regime saw behind Resolution 986.

14 Computed by the author from a report by the Iraqi Central Bank, broadcast on *Iraq TV Network,* February 9, 1996, in *FBIS-NES-DR,* February 13, 1996, pp. 30–32.

15 According to a reliable UN source who deals with Iraq, not only the government but also Saddam's family had control over the money-printing press—an additional reason why inflation went out of control. Based on author interview, May 26, 1998.

16 See *INA,* December 31, 1995, in *FBIS-NES-DR,* January 2, 1996, pp. 33–36; *al-Jumhuriyya,* December 17, 1995, in *FBIS-NER-DR,* March 19, 1996, p. 51.

17 From a report by the Iraqi Central Bank (see note 14); interviews with reporters who stayed in Baghdad in early 1996.

18 See *al-Jumhuriyya,* January 14 1996; *Alif Ba',* January 17, 1996, in *FBIS-NES-DR,* March 19, 1996, pp. 40–41. One kilogram of rice was ID 1,450; sugar, ID 1,800; cooking oil, ID 3,000; lentils, ID 2,000; beans, ID 2,700; a 850 gram can of tomato paste could reach ID 2,000; and half a kilogram of cheese, ID 1,600. An average monthly salary of a government official then was around ID 5,000.

19 See the *Reuters* news wire report, January 16, 1996, in *Gulf 2000* (an internet discussion group and documentation network managed by Gary Sick under the auspices of Columbia University), January 22, 1996.

20 See an interview with a senior Iraqi official, *Agence France Presse (AFP),* May 24, 1996, in *FBIS-NES-DR,* May 28, 1996, p. 32. This claim was confirmed in interviews with U.S. officials, Washington, D.C., August–September 1996. See also, for example, President Jacques Chirac confirming that "French diplomacy contributed to this agreement," *Radio Monte Carlo,* May 22, 1996, in *FBIS-NES-DR,* May 23, 1996, p. 14.

21 See *INA,* January 20, 1996, in *FBIS-NES-DR,* January 22, 1996, p. 25.

22 See *Reuters,* January 23, 1996, in *Gulf 2000,* January 24, 1996.

23 See *Iraq TV Network,* February 9, 1996, in *FBIS-NES-DR,* February 13, 1996, pp. 30–32.

24 UN Security Council, *Letter Dated 20 May 1996 from the Secretary General Addressed to the President of the Security Council: Memorandum of Understanding Between the Secretariat of the UN and the Government of Iraq on the Implementation of Security Council Resolution 986.* See Annex I, p. 11. See also Iraq's Oil Minister 'Amir Rashid al-Sa'di to *al-Hayat,* June 7, 1996, in *FBIS-NES-DR,* June 10, 1996, p. 23, pointing out that 440,000 bpd would be pumped to Turkey and 330,000 bpd through Mina Bakr on the Gulf.

25 Deputy Prime Minister Tariq Aziz, *Baghdad Iraq TV Network,* November 25, 1996, 18:00 GMT, in *FBIS-NES-DR-Serial JN2511203296,* November 25, 1996. Vice President Taha Yasin Ramadan, *Baghdad Iraq TV Network,* November 24, 1996, in *FBIS-NES-DR-Serial JN2411203696,* November 24, 1996.

26 *Baghdad Iraq TV Network,* November 26, 1996, in *FBIS-NES-DR-Serial JN2611190896,* November 26, 1996.

27 According to Iraqi statistical sources, in 1988, Iraq spent ID 671 million ($2.16 billion) on food imports. See Republic of Iraq, Ministry of Planning, Control Statistical Organization, *Annual Abstracts of Statistics, 1989* (Baghdad: Ministry of Planning, 1989), p. 220, table 8/4. In 1989, food imports increased substantially.

28 See *Ha'aretz,* February 17, 1997.

29 See *AP World Stream,* September 30, 1997.

30 See *Iraqi TV,* July 17, 1995, in *FBIS-NES-DR,* July 17, 1995, p. 38. See also Nizar Hamdun, *AFP,* July 19, 1995, in *FBIS-NES-DR,* July 20, 1995, p. 33.

31 An interview with a senior UN official, New York, October 13, 1995. See also UN Security Council *Note by the Secretary General: Annex: 9th Report of the Executive Chairman of the Special Commission on the Activities of the Special Commission* (New York: United Nations, June 20, 1995), pp. 4–6.

32 See *al-Ra'y,* November 26, 1997, in *FBIS-NES JN-2611206797,* November 27, 1997.

33 See *Reuters,* June 14, 1996, in *Gulf 2000,* June 14, 1996.

34 *White House News Wire,* July 9, 1996, in *Gulf 2000,* July 14, 1996. *Ha'aretz,* June 17, 23, 1996; *AFP* and *INA,* June 24, 1996, in *FBIS-NES-DR,* June 25, 1996, pp. 31–32.

35 See *Jordan Times,* July 18–19, 1996; *Ha'aretz,* July 21, 1996; *Reuters,* August 22, 1996; *AFP,* August 23, 1996.

36 See *Reuters,* November 22 and 25, 1996; President Clinton's letter, *U.S.*

Newswire, January 8, 1997. Only on February 22, 1997, did Iraq finally allow UNSCOM to remove the Scud rocket engines from the country.

37 See *Washington Post,* June 22, 1997, p. A26.

38 *Reuters,* October 6, 1997; *Financial Times,* October 8, 1997; Ian Black, *Guardian,* October 8, 1997.

39 See *AFP,* October 10, 1997.

40 See *New York Times,* October 31, 1997.

41 *Iraqi TV,* October 27, 1997, in *FBIS-NES-DR TN2710175097,* October 27, 1997.

42 Washington Kurdish Institute, quoting the news agencies, October 29, 1997.

43 Author interview with UN official, Washington, D.C., May 14, 1998, and telephone interview, June 25, 1998.

44 The anthem was written in 1981, after Saddam ousted his predecessor and became president. See also his Victory Day speech, *al-Thawra,* August 9, 1997.

45 It might be argued that if Saddam were to divulge all of his military secrets, with the new funds he would quickly amass from post-embargo oil sales and the extant knowledge of Iraq's weapons scientists, he could rebuild his unconventional arsenal very rapidly, and therefore, there is no reason for him to be so obstinate. Yet, this is not the case. Divulging such information so would betray important clandestine sources of material and procurement networks that he may not be able to reconstruct. Also, there are dual-use materials that Iraq acquired legally but cannot hope to get again (biological materials like anthrax growth material and chemical components).

46 For a detailed account, see Amatzia Baram, *Saddam's Iraq: Interplay Between Domestic Affairs and Foreign Policy* (Washington, D.C.: United States Institute of Peace, forthcoming).

47 See, for example, "A Letter from the President [Clinton] to the Speaker of the House of Representatives and the President Pro Tempore of the Senate, June 6, 1994" (Washington, D.C., Office of the Press Secretary, June 7, 1994), pp. 8–9. Secretary of State Madeleine Albright, in a speech on March 26, 1997, at Georgetown University, insisted that "the evidence is overwhelming that Saddam Husayn's intentions will never be peaceful," and because "Iraq must prove its peaceful intentions," it is only with a "successor regime" that the United States can enter into a dialogue. See, for example, *Iraqi Issues* 2, no. 1 (May 1997), pp. 6–7.

48 Bill Clinton, *News Hour with Jim Lehrer,* PBS, January 21, 1998.

Chapter 5

Ba'th versus Ba'th:
Iraq's Standing with Syria

Except for a few months in 1969–1970, seventeen days in 1973, and ten months in 1978–1979, relations between Ba'thi Iraq and Ba'thi Syria have always been tense. In the best of times, they have warmed to the level of a frosty political armistice, interrupted by salvoes of mutual abuse. In the worst of times, they have degenerated to the level of virulent hostility, featuring open military threats and war by proxy. Since the early days of the Iran–Iraq War, when Syria broke ranks with the other Arab states and cast its lot with Tehran, relations between Baghdad and Damascus have remained at the worst end of the spectrum.

This mutual hostility has applied not only to the regimes, but even more so to the two leaders. Although their competition for Arab leadership was one contributing factor to their animosity, the principal cause has been the domestic competition over Ba'thi legitimacy. Baghdad adopted the work of the Syrian Christian Michel 'Aflaq as its source of legitimacy, but Damascus championed the philosophy of the Syrian 'Alawi ideologue Zaki Arsuzi. This debate goes beyond differences in ideology, which are, after all, minute. Each regime sees the other as a threat to its legitimacy at home. Both regimes have a profound fear that domestic elements will adopt the causes of the other and use them as a rallying force against their own government. Indeed, both have gone to great lengths to foster violent, domestic opposition to the rival regime. Moreover, both have met with some success—not enough to topple the opposing regime, but more than enough to perpetuate the fear of "renegade" Ba'thi revolutionaries. This support has frequently gone beyond aiding political fellow travellers to supporting assassination attempts and mass revolts—Iraqi support for the Sunni Muslim Brotherhood in Syria, and Syrian support for Shi'i activists in Iraq. Saddam Husayn was personally in charge of both offensive activities in Syria and counterrevolutionary activities in Iraq in the 1970s, and this aggravated Syrian president Hafiz al-Asad's animosity toward him.

Relations hit rock bottom when Asad sent Syrian troops to join the forces of the coalition opposing Saddam during the Gulf War. This was a particularly telling gesture on Asad's part since most Syrians supported Saddam in the crisis. Syria contributed one division (the 9th Armored) to the coalition army, although this unit had orders only to aid a defense of Saudi Arabia and not to participate in an invasion of Kuwait—let alone Iraq. As emerges from interviews, U.S. officers were warned to watch their backs when they visited the Syrian cantonment, but, politically, the Syrian presence helped solidify the Arab coalition. Asad's decision to go to war with Iraq was evidence of his profound hatred and fear of Saddam: Rather than risk seeing Saddam victorious and a hero of the Arab masses, Asad decided to bite the bullet, join the "imperialist camp," and deal him a lethal blow. Another important motive for Asad was a desire to ingratiate himself with the world's only remaining superpower.

Only a few years after the Gulf War, a gradual change could be detected in Syria's position toward Iraq. The first sign of this came in negotiations over the water of the Euphrates river. As early as September 1992, representatives from Syria, Iraq, and Turkey met in Damascus to resume their prior discussions on a water-sharing agreement for the Euphrates.[1] Since then, Iraqi–Syrian teams have continued to meet regularly to discuss this issue. There are two reasons why these discussions have been continuing so smoothly despite the vitriolic rhetoric emanating from both capitals. In the first place, Euphrates water is such a crucial issue for both countries that it could not have been left unaddressed. The only alternative to negotiations was war (which almost erupted in the summer of 1975). Second, according to one Syria expert, Iraq and Syria essentially resolved their differences over the water issue in 1987. Yet, both continue to have problems with Turkey, and they recognize that it is much more effective for them to negotiate with Turkey jointly.[2] Another area in which the two countries have taken important cooperative steps is in energy production. In October 1996, the Iraqi parliament approved a draft agreement with Egypt, Jordan, Turkey, and Syria that would eventually link their electrical grids.[3]

More significantly, since mid-1996 Syria has gradually changed its public position on the fundamental issue of the struggle between Iraq and the United States. There is a strong sense in Damascus that the Syrian and Arab publics expect the Asad regime to support Iraq. But so far, Asad has been careful to do this only as long as such support cannot seriously enhance Saddam's position in Iraq, in the Arab world, or in the UN. When an Iraqi delegation participated in a regular meeting of the Arab Parliamentary Union held in Damascus, the president of Syria's parliament announced, for the first time ever, that Syria opposes the international sanctions against Iraq and that his country supports Iraq and its territorial integrity. In response, 'Udayy Saddam Husayn's *Babil* called for a quick rapprochement with Syria.[4] Damascus also supported Iraq during the Iraqi–U.S. confrontation in August–September 1996, denouncing the U.S. cruise missile strikes against Iraq. Baghdad's attempt to re-impose its rule over Iraqi Kurdistan was very popular with most Arabs and may explain the resounding Syrian condemnation of Washington. Syrian foreign minister Faruq al-Shara declared at that time that his country rejected any tampering with Iraq's territorial integrity and opposed the no-fly zones over northern and southern Iraq as well as Turkey's intent to establish a security zone in northern Iraq.[5] To date, this position has not changed. To prevent Jordanian political gains in a post-Saddam Iraq, Syria has also supported Iraq against King Hussein's plan to change the regime there.[6]

The signs of a budding *rapprochement* between Iraq and Syria increased considerably in 1997. In April, Iraq shut down the Syrian-opposition radio station "Voice of Arab Syria," which formerly had broadcast from Iraqi territory. This added impetus to Baghdad's efforts to diminish tension with Syria by ending its support for Syrian opposition groups, most notably closing the offices of the National Alliance for the Liberation of Syria the previous June.[7] With Iraq's acceptance of United Nations Security Council Resolution 986, the pace quickened. May 1997 saw an exchange of trade delegations between the two countries, which produced an Iraqi–Syrian agreement whereby Damascus would provide 50,000 tons of food products, grains, and detergent to Iraq for the price of $16.2 million. In June, Syria opened its border with Iraq in three places.[8] Later that month, Syrian vice president Abd al-Halim Khaddam reported that Damascus had reciprocated Baghdad's earlier goodwill gestures by limiting the activities of the anti-Iraq opposition groups based in the Syrian capital. Indeed, in mid-July, immediately after the first Syrian trucks unloaded their cargoes in

Baghdad, Syria closed down the anti-Baghdad radio station, Voice of Iraq. On July 24, 1997, the first Syrian tourists (since 1979) entered Iraq through the al-Bu Kamal border crossing, and five days later the first buses carrying Iraqi tourists left Baghdad for Damascus. Two weeks later, Syrian tourism minister Danhu Da'ud approved the establishment of the first Syrian–Iraqi tourism company, designed to run two daily trips between the two countries. By then, 5,000 Syrian businessmen had already applied for visas to Iraq to explore commercial opportunities, mainly in textiles and food products.[9] In mid-August, Syrian and Iraqi committees met in Baghdad to finalize the demarcation of several small strips along their border that had been left unresolved during their years of confrontation.[10]

During the summer, three unsual events provided occasions for the two countries to demonstrate further their improving relations. In late July, for the first time since 1980, Syrian companies had their own exhibition at Baghdad's trade fair. At the exhibition's gate the Iraqis allowed the Syrian delegation to display very conspicuously the portrait of President Asad alongside that of Saddam Husayn.[11] The significance of this gesture was not lost on anyone at the fair, for whom the animosity between Saddam and Asad had previously been taken as a permanent feature of the Middle Eastern landscape. "Sports diplomacy" was added to "portrait diplomacy" that same month, when a very large Iraqi athletic delegation went to Lebanon for the eighth Annual Pan-Arab games. Lebanese authorities stopped the ninety-seven athletes and accompanying personnel of the Iraqi team at the Syrian–Lebanese border in response to a Kuwaiti–Saudi protest. As both Riyadh and Kuwait had provided funding to rebuild Beirut's Sports City, this was not a demand the Lebanese felt they could refuse, but Damascus took full advantage of the event. Syria immediately took the Iraqis back, set them up in a posh hotel, and even permitted the delegation to display a portrait of Saddam Husayn on their buses as they traveled through Damascus.[12] The third event was cultural, with Iraq inviting Syrians to attend the annual Babylon International Festival. Syria accepted, even though the festival's theme that year was "From Nebuchadnezzar to Saddam, Babylon is Rising Again," and its purpose has traditionally been to emphasize Iraq's glory and seniority in the Arab family.[13]

The early autumn saw the relationship take an even more significant turn. On August 27, an Iraqi minister visited Damascus for the first time since 1979. Iraq's trade minister, Muhammad Mahdi Salih—Saddam's leading economic adviser—met with the Syrian deputy prime minister for economic affairs, Salim Yasin, Industry Minister Ahmad Nizam al-Din, and Minister of Transport Mufid Abd al-Karim.[14] Iraqi officials used the opportunity to announce that Baghdad planned to repair the old pipeline that had carried Iraqi oil from Haditha, Iraq, to Tartus, Syria, before the schism between the two regimes in the 1970s. Notably, the Syrians remained noncommittal on this initiative, in part because much of the Syrian part of the pipeline is already being used to deliver Syrian oil, and in part because Damascus always moves cautiously when major political shifts are involved.[15] Finally, in early September, an Iraqi delegation took part in a workshop organized by the Syrian Atomic Energy Commission.[16]

Syria's approach to its relationship with Iraq has gone through an intriguing metamorphosis. In June 1997, when the rapprochement began, Foreign Minister Shara implied on a number of occasions that normalization and full diplomatic relations were in the offing. During the same time frame, Syrian vice president Khaddam repeatedly implied that the relationship would likely even include strategic cooperation, casting the rapprochement as a response to deepening Turkish–Israeli ties. Syria argued that the budding alliance between Ankara and Jerusalem not only was intended to allow Syria's two most powerful enemies to coordinate their efforts against Damascus, but also was designed to enable Turkey to take over Iraq's Kirkuk oil fields and Israel to partition Iraq, force it into submission, and force it to accept Palestinian refugees.[17] Elsewhere, Khaddam explained that Syria's new policy toward Iraq was aimed at both preventing total Iraqi dependence on Turkey and foiling a plot to force Iraq to make peace with Israel.[18] According to one Syria analyst, part of the explanation for Syria's decision to normalize relations with Iraq lies in Asad's desire to demonstrate to Saudi Arabia that, unless it resumes its financial aid to Damascus, he will unlock the key to Saddam Husayn's jail cell. This tactic has already proven effective, spurring a surprise visit to Damascus by Saudi Crown Prince Abdullah and a promise that Riyadh would boycott the November 1997 Middle East/North Africa (MENA) Economic Conference in return for a Syrian pledge not to push for Iraq's rehabilitation.[19] It is not clear yet, however, whether Saudi Arabia will also foot Syria's bills.

Perhaps because Syria reaped some rewards early on, it later grew more cautious on the subject of Iraq. Apparently in response to Saudi–Kuwaiti pressures, Damascus explained that it had to measure its relations with Iraq "with a jeweler's scale," to avoid damaging Syria's relations with the Gulf states.[20] By the late summer of 1997, Syrian spokesmen were describing the turn toward Iraq in terms of their disappointment with the new intransigence of Israel's Netanyahu government.[21] Moreover, they claimed that the rapprochement was limited to the economic field.[22] It seems that, although the Israeli–Turkish limited alliance clearly troubled Syria, Damascus was still reluctant to antagonize its powerful northern neighbor more than was absolutely necessary. By contrast, Iraqi spokesmen made no secret of their intent to "buy" political recognition and normalization from Syria and other Arab states with long shopping lists of goods allowable under Resolution 986.[23]

These signs of warming should not yet be seen as a meaningful thaw, despite Baghdad's hopes. In all likelihood, Asad continues to favor maintaining sanctions on Iraq and is relying on the United States to keep them in place—no matter what Syrian propaganda may claim. Similarly, Asad appears to be counting on the Saudis and the Kuwaitis to bar any attempt to re-introduce Iraq into the Arab summits, despite Syria's indications that it wanted Iraq back there. For instance, Syria made no more than half-hearted efforts to push resolutions favoring Iraq at the last meeting of the "Damascus Declaration" states (the six Gulf Cooperation Council countries plus Egypt and Syria) which convened in the Syrian capital in June 1997. Indeed, the conference ended up reaffirming its traditional hard line on Iraq, yet Syria's *al-Ba'th* newspaper hailed its resolutions.[24] Along similar lines, Syrian spokesmen have consistently and unequivocally rejected 'Udayy's idea of a common Iraqi–Syrian–Iranian military front against Israel and Turkey.[25] In short, Asad currently has Saddam precisely where he wants him: Baghdad cannot threaten Damascus, and Saddam is now dependent on Syrian good offices. Asad's support for Iraq is for Arab and Syrian popular consumption, allowing him to burnish his image as an Arab nationalist. In addition, Asad hopes to secure lucrative trade deals with Iraq in return for his diplomatic support. Yet, if other Arab governments adopted the same approach, the embargo would disintegrate, even though none of the governments would actually like to see that happen.

In the past, warmer ties between Saddam and Asad have invariably been purely tactical moves. Whenever urgent political and strategic needs have dictated, the two regimes have shown that they can work together, if only for a short while. Thus in October 1973, Iraq sent two-thirds of its operational tank force to aid Syria in its war with Israel. Likewise, in 1978–1979, the two Ba'th regimes worked hand in hand against Sadat's Egypt and managed to build a large Arab anti-peace coalition. Today, the hostility and mistrust between the two leaders and their regimes is as intense as ever. The current rapprochement is no different, though, as both sides have purely selfish, and entirely tactical, motives. Syria hopes to use the threat of an Iraqi alliance as a source of leverage in its diplomatic efforts toward the Middle East peace process and the Turkish–Israeli alliance. For its part, Baghdad desperately needs Damascus to sponsor Iraq's rehabilitation within the Arab world. Baghdad has pressed Syria to go beyond mere economic ties and extend the rapprochement to diplomatic relations as well.[26] Such a development would be a major step forward on Iraq's road to seeing the United Nations sanctions lifted and its diplomatic isolation ended. Iraq may also have a more ambitious secondary agenda. Given the stalemate in the U.S.-sponsored Arab–Israeli peace process, Iraq may believe that a strong Syrian–Iraqi axis could undermine the Oslo accords and other peace negotiations, and instead foment renewed tensions and belligerency. Amid such chaos, Iraq could then assume a leading position as an Arab power and, if the United States wanted to restore the climate of peaceful negotiations, it would be compelled to seek Iraq's support—and pay the price for it.

The immediate benefits of a rapprochement with Syria should not suggest that this course is risk-free for Saddam. Compared to some other leading Iraqis (notably in the Foreign Office,) Saddam has been supportive but cautious in pursuing improved relations with Asad. So far he has never gone on record in favor of a rapprochement, leaving such statements to others. Apparently he needs to keep open a line of retreat in case Asad squelches the deal. For instance, 'Udayy has been pushing as hard as he can not only for an Iraqi–Syrian–Iranian rapprochement, but even for a common military front, possibly because it will open up new opportunities for graft and kickbacks. Like his father, Qusayy too may have reservations. Qusayy's responsibility is Iraq's internal security. An Iraqi–Syrian normalization will inevitably allow Syrian agents easier acces to Iraqi officials and army officers. Yet, Qusayy is not a political figure and cannot be expected to express his views politically either way.

Damascus has been even more hesitant. The best sign of this has been Syria's emphasis on symbolic cultural and economic actions and its careful avoidance of meaningful diplomatic ties. In fact, Syria has generally allowed its private sector to take the lead in relations with Iraq, reflecting the strong disincentives Asad continues to see regarding Iraq. First, as always in Syria, comes internal security. Asad must be careful that in improving his ties with Baghdad, he does not allow the Iraqis an opportunity to undermine his own hold on power. Asad is well aware that many Syrian

Sunnis are sympathetic to Saddam in the same way that many Iraqi Shi'a, as well as some Sunnis, are sympathetic toward Damascus. Of equal or greater importance, Asad must be careful that in putting pressure on the United States, Israel, Saudi Arabia, Kuwait, or Turkey, he does not alarm any of them and cause them to write off Syria as irredeemably belligerent. As long as he has reason to hope that Israeli–Syrian peace negotiations will resume, it is difficult to imagine that Asad would prefer an alliance with Iraq to peace with Israel. Such a choice could only isolate him in the Arab world and damage his relations with the United States, Saudi Arabia, and Kuwait. Thus, Iraq's desired radical front remains in political limbo.

Consequently, the most Asad is likely to do under the present circumstances is to improve his economic ties with Iraq (thereby reaping the additional benefit of punishing King Hussein by denying Jordan much-needed business with Iraq). As part of this course, Syria probably will also reopen its ports to Iraqi transit trade. Upgrading mutual diplomatic representation also seems a safe bet, but Asad will probably refrain from more meaningful political—and certainly military—cooperation, and he is unlikely to bust the embargo as Iraq wants him to do. Finally, Asad might consent to reopen the Iraqi–Syrian oil pipeline, but in addition to the technical difficulties, his incentive to do so has diminished as a result of the increase in Syria's own oil revenues. In 1996, Syrian oil revenues reached $2.5 billion (out of total exports of $4.5 billion), whereas the transfer fees from the Iraq pipeline are expected to reach only $100 million per year—not insignificant, but probably not enough to justify further angering Saudi Arabia, Kuwait, and the United States. Furthermore, most of the pipline's capacity is already being used by Syria itself to move its own oil to the Mediterranean coast.

The only events that could realistically propel Syria into Iraq's arms before the rest of the Arabs are ready to do the same would be a major crisis with Turkey, which seems far-fetched, or the ruination of the peace process, especially the Israeli–Palestinian track. If the peace process were to crumble and be replaced by a warlike atmosphere, Syria's incentives to avoid angering the Gulf states, the United States, and Israel will crumble with it. Indeed, Asad might consider it necessary to forge a new strategic alliance with Iraq to deter Israel or to build a war coalition. Security cooperation between these two might even include, if only symbolically, Syria's ally Iran as well. Such a tripartite coalition, even if beset by deep mistrust and hatred as seems inevitable, would still constitute a major negative change in the political atmosphere throughout the Middle East.

NOTES

1   See *al-Hayat,* September 29, 1992, p. 4.

2   Water Experts Committee member Ambassador Muhammad Munib al-Rifa'i, in a meeting in Baghdad, *Iraqi News Agency (INA),* July 6, 1996, in *Foreign Broadcast Information Service–Near East and South Asia–Daily Report (FBIS-NES-DR),* July 8, 1996, pp. 21–22.

3   *INA,* October 28, 1996, in *FBIS-Serial JN2810214596,* October 28, 1996.

4   For the Syrian parliamentarian's declaration, see news agencies as quoted in *al-Malaff al-'Iraqi,* no. 54 (June 1996), p. 36; see also *Reuters* from Baghdad, May 16, 1996, quoting Speaker of the Syrian Parliament 'Abd al-Qadir Kaddur telling an Iraqi parliamentary delegation in Damascus that the trade embargo could not be supported and that Syria was supportive of Iraq's "territorial integrity," in *Gulf 2000* (an internet discussion group and documentation network managed by Gary Sick under the auspices of Columbia University), May 17, 1996. For *Babil,* see *Reuters,* May 19, 1996, in *al-Malaff al-'Iraqi,* no. 54 (June 1996), p. 36.

5   *Mideast Mirror,* September 17, 1996; *Washington Times,* September 4, 1996; *Reuters* from London, September 3, 1996.

6   Faruq al-Shara, quoted in *INA,* November 27, 1996, in *FBIS-Serial JN2711125896,* November 27, 1996.

7   See *BBC Monitor in World Media,* report of June 27, 1997, as to which opposition stations have been broadcasting and since when.

8   See *Xinhua,* May 25, 1997, *UPI,* May 30, 1997, and *Radio Monte Carlo,* June 2, 1997, in *BBC Summary of World Broadcasts (BBC–SWB),* June 4, 1997; see also *Reuters World Service,* June 9, 1997; *Deutche Presse Agentur,* June 14, 1997; *Iraqi TV,* July 7, 1997; and *UPI,* June 13, 1997. *INA,* on August 31, 1997, reported the value of the trade to be $20 million.

9   *Syrian Arab News Agency (SANA),* June 14, 1997, reporting Khaddam's interview in *al-Quds al-'Arabi,* in *BBC–SWB,* June 17, 1997; *al-Sharq al-Awsat,* July 24, 1997, in *BBC–SWB,* August 1, 1997; *Voice of Rebellious Iraq,* July 30, 1997, in *BBC–SWB,* August 1, 1997; *Radio Monte Carlo,* August 4, 1997, in *BBC–SWB,* August 12, 1997; for Syrian businessmen, see *INA,* August 7, 1997, in *BBC–SWB,* August 12, 1997.

10   *Agence France Presse (AFP),* August 14, 1997.

11   *Associated Press (AP) World Stream,* July 27, 1997.

12   *Mideast Mirror,* July 14, 1997, p. 14, 15; *AFP,* July 28, 1997; *UPI,* August 17, 1997.

13 *AFP,* September 22, 1997. For the function of the Babylon Festival, see Amatzia Baram, *Culture, History, and Ideology in the Formation of Ba'thist Iraq 1968–1989* (New York: St. Martin's Press, 1991), pp. 47–50.

14 *Iraqi TV,* August 28, 1997, in the *BBC–SWB,* September 2, 1997; *AP,* August 27, 1997.

15 *Financial Times,* August 20, 1997; *Deutsche Presse Agentur,* August 19, 1997; *al-Hayat,* August 24, 1997; an interview with an oil executive, Washington D.C., November 1997.

16 See *al-Hayat,* quoting official Syrian sources, September 8, 1997.

17 See, for example, *TASS,* June 9, 1997; *AFP,* June 20, 1997. See also Khaddam in *Mideast Mirror,* June 18, 1997.

18 *Reuters* from Damascus, June 18, 1997, in *al-Malaff al-'Iraqi,* no. 67 (July 1997), p. 3. According to the Saudi-sponsored *al-Sharq al-Awsat,* in a meeting between Abd al-Halim Khaddam, Syria's vice president, and Iran's outgoing president, Ali Akbar Hashemi Rafsanjani, the former explained the recent Syrian–Iraqi raprochement as resulting from the dangerous Turkish–Israeli alliance. See *Ha'aretz,* June 20, 1997.

19 Zuhayr Diyab, *Mideast Mirror,* September 19, 1997. See also *Mideast Mirror,* June 30, 1997, p. 15.

20 *al-Hayat,* July 30, 1997, in *BBC–SWB,* August 1, 1997.

21 Khaddam to *al-Sharq al-Awsat,* July 24, 1997, in *BBC–SWB,* July 26, 1997.

22 Foreign Minister Shara, *al-Hayat,* October 3, 1997, in *BBC–SWB,* October 7, 1997; a senior Syrian official (possibly Shara), *AFP,* August 29, 1997. In the latter report there is also evidence for Kuwaiti pressure.

23 For example, Foreign Minister Muhammad Said al-Sahhaf in Cairo, *Middle East News Agency (MENA),* September 22, 1997, in *BBC–SWB,* September 24, 1997.

24 *Mideast Mirror,* June 26, 1997, pp. 12–14.

25 See, for example, *al-Hayat,* August 24, 1997; the news agencies from Baghdad, as reported in *al-Malaff al-'Iraqi,* no. 67 (July 1997), p. 3. For an early rejection by Shara, see *AFP,* June 20, 1997.

26 See, for example, Sa'd Qasim Hammudi, head of the Iraqi parliament's Foreign Affairs Comittee, calling Syria to restore full diplomatic relations, *TASS,* June 6, 1997.

Chapter 6

Iraq's Great Eastern Neighbor: Iran

Since the end of the Iran–Iraq War in 1988, negotiations have become a staple of Iraq's relationship with its great eastern neighbor. Although they have graduated to the level of ministerial-level visits, these negotiations have resolved very little.[1] Although on the face of it both sides have strong incentives to resolve their differences—both having been declared pariah states by the United States and in need of support from every possible source—the two sides have been unable to get past their mutual suspicions and hatreds. Whenever the two countries seem to be approaching a diplomatic breakthrough, something happens that pushes all efforts at reconciliation back to square one. For example, in October 1994, a visit by Iran's foreign minister, Ali Akbar Velayati, to Baghdad was agreed upon, only to be aborted following an Iranian mortar attack on a camp of Iraqi-backed Iranian *Mujahidin e-Khalq* (MEK).[2] Nevertheless, the fact that the two parties allow secondary considerations to derail major diplomatic initiatives may serve as evidence that neither considers rapprochement a priority, and to a certain extent, rivalry is more useful to both than reconciliation.

There are a number of bones of contention that haunt Iraqi–Iranian relations, each of which alone is usually sufficient to wreck any progress toward a settlement. One is the 148 airplanes (115 of them warplanes) that Iraq sent to Iran during the Gulf War. According to a very reliable U.S. military source, several dozen crashed, but the rest landed safely at Iranian airfields. As could be expected, the Iranians insist that only twenty-two actually reached their airspace. Iraq demands the return of these aircraft, which included many of the country's most advanced strike aircraft—all of its Soviet-made Su-24 attack jets and nearly all of its Mirage F-1EQ5/6 fighter-bombers. Iran cleverly turned to the United Nations for a ruling and, conveniently, was forbidden to send them back because under UN Security Council Resolution 661 they are considered part of Iraq's frozen assets.[3]

Another issue that divides Iran and Iraq is the dispute over the remaining prisoners of war (POWs) from the Iran–Iraq War. Until the most recent exchange in April 1998, Iran claimed that Iraq still held 5,000 Iranian POWs and that it returned all Iraqi POWs (more than 47,000 of them). Iraq was equally adamant that there were still 20,000 Iraqi POWs in Iranian hands—including 10,000 who want to stay in Iran, according to Iranian authorities.[4] Iraq also insists that it returned all 39,043 Iranian POWs by August 18, 1990 (as a gesture of friendship, after Baghdad's annexation of Kuwait antagonized the rest of the world), and that only one prisoner remained: an Iranian pilot who bombed Iraq before the Iraqi offensive of September 1985.[5] In early April 1988 the two countries exchanged prisoners of war for the second time. This was, apparently, the result of discussions between an Iraqi delegation to the December 1997 Organization of the Islamic Conference (OIC) summit in Tehran—which included Vice President Taha Yasin Ramadan and Foreign Minister Muhammad Sa'id al-Sahhaf—and Iran's President Muhammad Khatemi and Foreign Minister Kamal Kharrazi. The Iranians returned 5,592 Iraqi prisoners in exchange for 380 Iranians.[6] Still, it is not yet clear whether this last exchange effectively resolves the prisoners issue; after all, both sides are on record claiming that the other side has many more prisoners it refuses to return. Most probably, many prisoners died in captivity and that their deaths were never reported to the Red Cross, whereas each country still considers these individuals to be prisoners of the other country. Moreover, some Western intelligence officers believe Iran recruited Shi'i Iraqi POWs to both the Badr brigade of the Supreme Alliance of the Islamic Republic of Iran (SAIRI) and various intelligence and sabotage organs working outside of Iran for the Iranian government; it is highly unlikely that any of these will be returned to Iraq. Thus, although the POW issue seems to have lost much weight in bilateral relations, the fact that individuals remain "missing" means that one of the sides might still bring it up again as a high-profile issue.

Several other disputes divide Iran and Iraq and regularly force the suspension of their efforts at reconciliation. The two armies continue to stumble into small-scale border clashes that often occur over the most minor issues—or for no apparent reason at all. Sovereignty over the Shatt al-Arab remains an outstanding bone of contention. In addition, Iraq has issued both public and diplomatic complaints about Iranian designs on Bahrain and its continued occupation of the Gulf islands of Greater and Lesser Tunb and Abu Musa, which the Arabs contend rightfully belong to the United Arab Emirates.[7]

Moreover, despite their fumbling negotiations, both countries continue actively to support armed opposition groups. Baghdad provides low-level support to some Iranian Kurdish groups and other ethnic opposition organizations. Of greatest importance, however, Iraq effectively controls the Iranian MEK, furnishing it with all the accoutrements of a modern army and encouraging it to stage hit-and-run operations into Iran whenever Saddam Husayn wants to put pressure on Tehran. Baghdad supports a division-sized force of the MEK at Khalis, east of Baghdad along the Iranian border. Over the last six years, MEK raids have provoked Iran to respond by sending agents to sabotage MEK installations in Baghdad. Occasionally, Iran has even sent troops and warplanes into Iraq to hit the MEK bases.[8] The last such confrontation occured on September 29, 1997, when four Iranian F-4 fighter-bombers hit the main MEK camp in retaliation for an MEK raid. Baghdad sent up its own fighters ostensibly to intercept the Iranian jets, thus violating the southern no-fly zone. This, in turn, provoked the United States to accelerate the deployment of the aircraft carrier *U.S.S. Nimitz* to the Gulf as a warning to Iraq. Iran's ambassador to the UN informed the secretary general that Iran sees it as its right to retaliate against Iraq for MEK attacks. Iraq's *al-Jumhuriyya* reacted ferociously by promising "two blows for every blow,"[9] and the MEK in Baghdad vowed to continue its activities to "overthrow the Iranian regime."[10] This military skirmish derailed an important meeting between the two foreign ministers that had been scheduled to take place in New York just three days later.[11]

For its part, Iran supports some Iraqi Kurdish Islamists as well as Jalal Talabani's anti-regime PUK in the North (in 1995 Iran supported Mas'ud Barzani's KDP, but in 1996 it switched its backing to the PUK). Although Iran has provided Talabani with some arms, money, sanctuary, logistical support, training, and even advisers, it has generally refrained from committing Iranian combat troops to the fighting in Iraqi Kurdistan. The most important exception to this rule was Tehran's insertion of considerable numbers of Iranian Revolutionary Guards into Kurdistan during the summer of 1996, although even then these units stayed in Iraq for only a few days. Nevertheless, the direct Iranian intervention allowed the Iraqi regime to claim this was an Iranian invasion and a danger to the territorial integrity of Iraq that justified a direct Iraqi military response, even in Kurdish lands previously forbidden to Iraqi military forces. Thus, the Iranian presence helped Saddam justify his attack on Irbil, but in so doing he set back the diplomatic clock with Tehran, as it created an atmosphere that rendered any negotiations impossible. Most disconcerting to Baghdad, however, has been Iran's steady support for Shi'i guerrillas operating in southern Iraq and the capital itself. In addition to the immediate threat this support poses to Saddam's undisputed rule, Iran's involvement with the Shi'a serves as a constant reminder of the Shi'i *intifada* (uprising) of March 1991, which received limited support from Tehran and was the most dangerous moment for Saddam's regime. As Saddam bitterly noted in 1997, the Iranians stabbed Iraq with "the sharpest daggers of treachery" when they supported the insurrection.[12]

Even the occasional gestures of goodwill from either side are more often intended as concealed barbs. For instance, in a surprise unilateral gesture, Saddam opened the Iraqi border to Iranian pilgrims on September 4, 1997. Two of the holiest sites in Shi'i Islam—Najaf and Karbala—are in central Iraq, and Saddam announced that for the very reasonable fee of $500, Iranian Shi'a could spend a week visiting their holy places. Saddam made it clear that this gesture was designed to humiliate the Iranian regime. First, the announcement came only days after he lambasted Iran for killing and torturing Iraqi POWs and for preventing the remaining ones from returning home. In this same speech, he declared that the Iranian leadership is not Shi'i at all. He claimed that in fact, they (and, by implication, the late Ayatollah Ruhollah Khomeini) have always been heretics who hate Islam and the Arabs.[13] Against this backdrop, he sent fifty buses to the border, each carrying the slogan, "We welcome Iranians to Iraq, country of the Pious Saddam." It was not lost on anyone that the date Baghdad chose to begin this pilgrimage is the date the Iraqis claim Iran started the Iran–Iraq War in 1980. To add insult to injury, Iraq announced that in return for Baghdad's generous gesture, it expected Tehran to release all of the Iraqi POWs, return Iraqi aircraft, and agree to a policy of mutual "noninterference in [each other's] internal affairs." Iranian police immediately blocked the Iraqi embassy in Tehran and barred entry to those Iranians who came for visas for the pilgrimage.[14] As Saddam had hoped, the clerics ruling in

Tehran were deeply embarrassed, and they lashed out at Baghdad for cynically playing with the religious sentiments of the Iranian people, when they actually had no intention of making good on their promises.[15] Iran, for its part, sent humanitarian supplies to Iraq a few times, as a sign of Islamic solidarity with the Iraqi people.

Indeed, more than signs of good intent, these gestures are signs of the battle between Baghdad and Tehran for the hearts and minds of the people on both sides of their border. Tehran cannot ignore the sympathy Iranians feel toward the plight of their coreligionists in Iraq as a result of the embargo, and it hopes also to rekindle the pro-Iranian sentiments of the Iraqi Shi'a. Baghdad hopes to demonstrate to its own Shi'a, as well as to the Iranian people (most of whom are Shi'a), its respect for their religious obligations such as pilgrimage, thus undermining public support for Shi'i theocracy in both Iran and Iraq. All the same, Saddam's initiative makes it easier than before for both sides to cooperate over future pilgrimages: Iraq will have a difficult time changing its new policy, and Iran will be under great public pressure to reverse its previous policy.

Frequent expressions of desire for a rapprochement notwithstanding, the most that the two countries have managed to achieve so far were agreements in two fields. A memorandum of understanding signed on September 14, 1995, specifies guidelines for the exchange of the remains of fallen soldiers.[16] Formal agreements on the exchange of bodies are usually a gesture between two warring sides and odd for states nominally attempting to improve relations. Tehran and Baghdad have also managed a limited level of practical cooperation over the very minimal navigation on the Shatt al-Arab. The question of sovereignty remains unresolved, but the Iraqis nonetheless dredged the waterway and the Iranians turned a blind eye. Today both sides use the waterway without incident.

Prior to 1998, Iran and Iraq had also managed a highly beneficial cooperation smuggling Iraqi oil. The United States repeatedly reported that Iran allowed small oil tankers to sail in its territorial waters from Iraq to the United Arab Emirates, thus enabling the smugglers to avoid U.S. warships enforcing the blockade of Iraq. Reportedly, a Revolutionary Guard post at the mouth of the Shatt al-Arab served as the point where payments were collected for this passage. The former commander of the Maritime Interdiction Force estimated that 60,000 tons of oil per month were smuggled through this route. At $75 per metric ton, this amounted to around $54 million annually.[17] President Bill Clinton reported that "elements within the Iranian government" were extracting "protection fees" from the smugglers.[18] Tehran denied these allegations,[19] but in November 1996, Iraqi finance minister Hikmat Ibrahim al-'Azzawi declared, "Smuggling is one way of trading; . . . [the smuggling agency] has contacts with the central government."[20] Indeed, the UN Sanctions Committee admonished Iran for its support of the smuggling.[21] Yet, in the second half of 1997, the quantity of oil smuggled through Iranian territorial waters almost doubled. Things changed dramatically in early 1998, when Iran shut down this profitable cooperation to a large extent, but in April the smuggling operation was completely back on track, after Iran secured an increase in "protection fees" from the relevant Iraqi authority. This is yet another sign that Iran's cooperation with Iraq is purely mercenary and will cease quickly whenever Tehran changes its mind.

Mutual relations between Iraq and Iran are thus still fraught with deep mutual mistrust, painful memories, and numerous friction points which can easily become flash points. Another all-out war between the two is highly unlikely: Both countries realize that they cannot win, and a new war will only bring mutual devasatation. Yet, their ongoing frictions probably will continue to spark local skirmishes and a meaningful rapprochement is not in the offing. Consequently, at present, having the other as a reliable scapegoat is important to both regimes, which explains the reluctance on the part of either Baghdad or Tehran to forgo attacks on each other or cease support for the other's militant opposition movements. It also explains the willingness of both sides to accuse each other of acts of sabotage that almost certainly were perpetrated by indigenous forces: Iran accused Iraq of setting off a bomb at the Imam Reza Shrine in Mashhad in June 1994, and Iraq accused Iran of the assassination attempt on 'Udayy Saddam Husayn in December 1996. In both cases, all diplomatic contacts once again ground to a halt for months afterward.

Is a rapprochement possible soon? It seems unlikely, but surprises have been a long-standing feature of the Iran–Iraq relationship. The 1975 Algiers Accord between Saddam and the Shah came as a surprise to the rest of the world, especially given the atmosphere of rhetorical attacks and border skirmishes that preceded it. Moreover, despite the constant breakdowns in their negotiations, both sides repeatedly intone that they are seeking improved relations. The last such vows were heard in December 1997 during the OIC summit in Tehran, when Iraqi vice president Taha Yasin Ramadan met with Iranian president Muhammad Khatemi. The Iranian President asked Ramadan to convey greetings to Saddam Husayn and the two leaders "agreed on means of settling the pending issues."[22] Thus, a surprise agreement cannot be ruled out. Yet, the rivers of bad blood between them, the litany of grievances each holds against the other, and the present thinking of the sides suggest that a comprehensive accommodation is still years away. Much more likely is an incremental agreement that solves the outstanding issues gradually, one-by-one.

When the rivals at long last decide that a good (or tolerable) neighbor is more beneficial than a reliable enemy they will have to resolve at least one intractable issue: sovereignty over the Shatt. This will not be easy, as it involves the reputation and national honor of Iran and Iraq. Sovereignty over the Shatt is largely a theoretical issue right now, because both sides currently use the waterway without incident. But this does not mean it will be easily resolved. For Iran, conceding to Iraq on the Shatt will be an admission that Saddam was right in 1980 when he declared the 1975 agreement null and void—an act that precipitated by five days the Iraqi offensive that started the Iran–Iraq War. For Saddam, conceding to Iran would mean admitting that he was wrong when he went to war, in part over the issue of the sovereignty of the Shatt. Consequently, the staggering costs of the war—one million dead, hundreds of billions of dollars wasted, and eight years of excruciating war—will serve to prevent either side from compromising. Because both regimes probably would prefer to leave this issue untouched well into the next millennium, they are unlikely to make serious efforts toward a formal peace agreement that would, of necessity, have to address this dispute. Yet, a series of practical arrangements short of formal peace is possible, even with no reference to the issue of sovereignty.

The POW issue, which until recently also seemed intractable, seems to have been solved, but both sides have yet to announce that all their demands have been met. As long as this is the case, the prisoners' file is not closed.

The opposition groups, by contrast, probably would not be an insurmountable obstacle to an Iranian–Iraqi rapprochement. This is not to say they are unimportant: For both sides, the opposition groups are useful tools with which to prod their rival. Saddam, in particular, has always combined the carrot and the stick, and he does not believe in unilateral gestures like the dismantling of the MEK's small army. The MEK is a very useful stick that, as Saddam sees it, is not to be disposed of lightly. Yet, once Saddam feels a compelling need to end or freeze the feud with Iran, he can demonstrate his goodwill by freezing the MEK's activities for a test-period. Ultimately, there can be little doubt that if Saddam can get a deal he likes from Iran, he will be willing to sacrifice the MEK, although even then he may continue to support them, just in case the situation again changes. For political and ideological reasons, it will be much easier for Saddam to muzzle the MEK than for the Iranians to do the same to the Iraqi–Shi'i opposition. Nevertheless, the Iranians too will likely agree to rein in their proxies in return for an agreement with Iraq they found beneficial.

Given that a full rapprochement with Tehran is probably not in the offing, Baghdad cannot expect much help from Tehran. Saddam can expect continued, low-level smuggling through Iran in violation of the international embargo. Iran can cite the dispensations that the UN has granted to both Turkey and Jordan and demand the same treatment so that they can continue their profitable smuggling operations. Still, there is little chance that Iran will risk having the UN slap sanctions on it for gross violations of the embargo on Iraq.[23] The unspoken agreement on the Shatt al-Arab that currently prevails benefits both sides and thus is unlikely to be challenged. Iraq can probably expect that if the Arab–Israeli peace process were to crumble, Iran would be ready for joint diplomatic action against the United States and Israel in the UN and Islamic organizations. On the other hand, Saddam must assume that Iran will continue its covert activities in Kurdistan and in southern Iraq, as well as its attacks on MEK targets in Baghdad and elsewhere in Iraq.

What should be most worrying to Saddam, however, is the fact that the Iranian regime is content with the present situation in Iraq. Tehran greatly benefits from an Iraqi regime bound by sanctions, with very limited revenue, with almost no ability to re-arm, and whose air force is largely grounded. Because Iran is not subject to the same military and economic limitations, the Iranians have a breathing space in which to rebuild their armed forces. Similarly, as Iran is an oil-producing country, limitations on Iraqi oil exports are a blessing to Tehran.[24] At the same time, Iranian pragmatists—including Khatemi and former President Ali Akbar Hashemi Rafsanjani—are not eager to see Saddam Husayn's downfall. They may fear that his overthrow could lead to the disintegration of Iraq, a massive refugee problem, and an Afghanistan style chaos that could induce Iranian radicals to intervene at least in the Shi'i South, thus bringing Iran into conflict with the Arab world and the West. Likewise, the fear that Saddam's successor would be a pro-Western regime gives Iranian radicals pause. It is therefore likely that many in Tehran agree that the preservation of the status quo in Iraq is the best of all possible worlds for Iran.

Still, Saddam's compelling need for diplomatic allies will probably lead him to be somewhat more accommodating of Iran. For example, in the case of a military confrontation between Israel and Syria, Baghdad would probably allow a limited number of Iranian Revolutionary Guards and military supplies to cross into Syria through Iraq. Iraq would probably also agree to rein in the MEK in return for proof that Iran had ceased all support to Iraq's frustrating Shi'i, marsh Arab, and Kurdish insurgencies. Moreover, Iraq is ready to sell considerable amounts of oil to Iran at reduced prices, although Iran so far has been unwilling to allow more than limited smuggling along its coastline, for fear that doing more would incur U.S. and UN wrath. Finally, seen from an Iraqi viewpoint, any rapprochement between Iran and the United States is cause for concern. Thus, the Iraqi regime may be expected to offer Iran small concessions to try to dissuade it from making peace with the Clinton administration.

NOTES

1   *Iraqi News Agency (INA)* and *Islamic Republic News Agency (IRNA)*, February 17, 1994, in *Foreign Broadcast Information Service–Near East and South Asia–Daily Report (FBIS-NES-DR)*, February 17, 1994, pp. 20, 44; *INA*, May 28, 1996, in *FBIS-NES-DR*, May 30, 1996, pp. 31–32; *Reuters* from Baghdad, May 26, 1995; and *Reuters* from Tehran, May 28, 1995. The last such ministerial-level visit, as of June 1998 was that of the Iranian minister of health, Reza Marandi, who met with Iraq's foreign minister, Muhammad al-Sahhaf, in Baghdad on June 22, 1997, and invited Iraq to participate in the meeting of the Organization of the Islamic Conference in Tehran, which took place in December 1997. Senior Iraqi politicians and officials then participated in the OIC and met with Iranian president Muhammad Khatemi and others.

2   *Reuters* from Tehran, May 22, 1995.

3   *Deutsche Presse Agentur,* September 23, 1997.

4   *IRNA*, July 25, 1995, in *FBIS-NES-DR*, July 26, 1995, p. 27; also *INA*, February 17, 1994, in *FBIS-NES-DR,* February 17, 1994, p. 20; *INA*, May 28, 1996, *FBIS-NES-DR,* May 30, 1996, pp. 31–32.

5   The one remaining "prisoner" was a pilot whose Phantom jet fighter was downed in mid-September 1980, and he is kept in Iraq as living proof that Iran started the war. See Saddam's Victory Day speech, *Iraqi TV,* August 8,

1997, in *BBC Summary of World Broadcasts (BBC–SWB),* August 11, 1997. See also, *al-Thawra,* August 7, 1997, in *Agence France Presse (AFP),* August 17, 1997. In April 1998, however, he was returned.

6   See *New York Times,* April 7, 1998; *INA,* December 12, 1997, in *FBIS-NES-97-346 NC1212114397,* December 12, 1997. Most of the Iranians returned by Baghdad were not prisoners of war from the IranIraq War but, rather, Iranians captured during the suppression of the Shi'i *intifada* (uprising) in southern Iraq in March–April 1991.

7   See, for example, Sa'd Qasim Hammudi, chairman of the Arab and International Relations Committee of the National Assembly, in *INA,* June 6, 1996, in *FBIS-NES-DR,* June 7, 1996, p. 21; *al-Thawra,* June 6, 1996.

8   See report by the Mujahidin to the United Nations, according to which the Iranians launched against them thirty-four attacks between 1993 and July 1995. *AFP,* July 9, 1995, in *FBIS-NES-DR,* July 10, 1995, pp. 50–51. See also the report by *Reuters* from Tehran, May 22, 1995, according to which a visit of Iranian foreign minister Ali Akbar Velayati was planned for October 1994 but cancelled as a result of an Iranian mortar attack on the Mujahidin.

9   For the Iranian letter see *IRNA,* October 4, 1997; *Chicago Tribune,* October 13, 1997; *Washington Times,* October 11, 1997; *AFP,* October 6, 1997; *al-Jumhuriyya,* October 6, 1996.

10 *AFP,* October 1, 1997.

11 *AFP,* October 5, 1997.

12 *Iraqi TV,* August 8, 1997, in *BBC–SWB,* August 11, 1997. See also, *al-Thawra,* August 7, 1997, in *AFP,* August 7, 1997.

13 Saddam's Victory Day speech, *Iraq TV Network,* August 8, 1997, in *FBIS-NES-DR,* August 8, 1997.

14 *AFP,* September 4, 1997. *Babil,* August 19, 1997, in *BBC–SWB,* August 27, 1997; *AFP,* August 26, 1997. See also comments from Iraq's Ministry of the Interior to *INA,* August 28, 1997, in *AFP,* August 28, 1997; *Associated Press (AP),* August 29, 1997.

15 *Vision of the Islamic Republic of Iran Network 1,* August 27, 1997, in *BBC–SWB,* August 29, 1997; *Voice of the Islamic Republic of Iran,* August 28, 1997, in *BBC–SWB,* August 30, 1997.

16 *INA,* June 25, 1996, in *FBIS-NES-DR,* June 26, 1996, p. 30.

17 See *al-Jumhuriyya,* June 13, 1993.

18 See Vice Adm. Thomas B. Fargo to *AP,* February 11, 1997; President Bill Clinton's letter to the Speaker of the House of Representatives and the

President Pro Tempore of the Senate, *U.S. Newswire,* January 8, 1997.

19 *Reuters,* February 11, 1997.

20 Interview of Iraqi finance minister Hikmat Ibrahim al-'Azzawi, by Roula Khalaf in Baghdad, *Financial Times,* November 9, 1996, in *Gulf 2000* (an internet discussion group and documentation network managed by Gary Sick under the auspices of Columbia University), November 13, 1996.

21 President Clinton's letter, *U.S. Newswire,* January 8, 1997.

22 See *INA,* December 12, 1997, in *FBIS-NES-97-346 NC1212114397,* December 12, 1997. See also Khatemi's congratulatory Ramadan message to Saddam in *al-Ra'y,* January 2, 1998.

23 In an interview, Tariq 'Aziz admitted that, on a visit to Tehran after the invasion of Kuwait, he offered the Iranians cheap oil products, which they were buying at a very high cost, if they were ready to ignore the embargo, but they turned him down. *Baghdad Observer,* March 16, 1992.

24 See some of these views expressed by parliamentary Foreign Relations Committee member (and Iran's ambassador to the UN, 1984–1990) Sa'id Raja'i Khorasani, *UPI,* May 24, 1995.

Chapter 7

Looking Northward: Turkey

Baghdad has generally been of two minds when it looks northward.[1] On the one hand, Turkey is a North Atlantic Treaty Organization (NATO) ally of the United States. It is desperate to join the European Union, it has faithfully supported Western diplomatic and military moves in the Gulf region, and it allowed United Nations (UN) coalition forces to use Turkish bases to stage strikes against Iraq throughout the Gulf War. On the other hand, Ankara and Baghdad have a number of common interests, including mutual economic relations and similar difficulties with their respective Kurdish populations. Turkish–Iraqi relations were very good until the Gulf War: Turkey profited considerably from Iraqi oil exported from Turkey via the Kirkuk–Dortyol pipeline, both sides enjoyed the benefits of considerable trade, and they frequently cooperated against each other's Kurdish opposition groups. Moreover, Turkey has been relatively benign toward Iraq since the Gulf War. Ankara was uncomfortable with Operation Provide Comfort and has been ambivalent about the ongoing Northern Watch missions being flown by American and British (and, until recently, French) warplanes from Turkish bases and has attempted to limit or even kill the operation. Turkey has placed severe limitations on U.S. Air Force activities from the Incirlik base. Turkey has allowed large-scale semilegal oil transfers across its border. It has repeatedly stated that it wants to resume broad economic relations with Iraq, and it was among the first to line up at Baghdad's door for trade deals once the Iraqis accepted UN Security Council Resolution 986. Turkish officials regularly complain that Turkey has been losing some $6 billion to $7 billion annually because of the embargo, including $250 million annually for pipeline fees.[2] Consequently, although Saddam must still consider Turkey as a U.S. ally, he also sees it as a potential defector from the U.S.-led coalition and—in some ways—even as a potential ally for Baghdad.

For its part, three principal interests guide Turkey's foreign policy toward Iraq. First, Ankara wants to prevent the emergence of a Kurdish state, even within the borders of Iraq alone, for fear that this would jeopardize Turkish control over its own Kurdish territories. Second, the Turks are determined to stop PKK infiltration from Iraqi Kurdistan into Turkey. Finally, the Turkish economy has greatly benefited from trade with Iraq and from transhipment fees for Iraqi oil pumped through the Kirkuk–Dortyol pipeline. A host of other considerations—relations with the United States and its other NATO allies, relations with the Gulf Cooperation Council (GCC) states, and preventing an aggressive and unpredictable neighbor from acquiring weapons of mass destruction—also crowd Turkish decision making on Iraq, but, save its relations with the United States, they are not Ankara's primary motives. What is obvious from this list is that Turkey's priorities with Iraq are—as Baghdad ardently believes—issues on which the two countries are in full agreement, and which suggest the need for cooperation between the two capitals, not confrontation.

With this in mind, Iraq has waged a full-scale diplomatic offensive to coax Turkey into closer relations. Mindful of Ankara's frustration over Kurdistan Workers' Party (PKK) infiltration and Turkey's economic losses since the Kuwait crisis, Iraqi spokesmen have tirelessly called upon Ankara to help Baghdad reassert its control over northern Iraq, stop the embargo, and reestablish mutual trade. Baghdad has promised to neutralize the PKK once Iraq is again in control of Kurdistan. Upon his arrival in Ankara in September 1993, Iraqi trade minister Muhammad Mahdi Salih reportedly offered Turkey 100,000 barrels of crude oil per day free of charge, in addition to a $4 per barrel transit fee, if Turkey would agree to break the sanctions by allowing Iraq to export oil through Ceyhan.[3] Baghdad has also tried to use the possibility of reopening the Syrian–Iraqi pipeline and even threatened to build a new pipeline to Aqaba, Jordan—and so render Iraq less dependent on the Turkish pipeline—if Ankara is not more accommodating of Iraqi interests.[4] In particular, Iraq has demanded that Turkey put an end to Operation Provide Comfort (since 1996 renamed Operation Northern Watch), the coalition air missions that enforce the northern no-fly zone.[5]

Under President Turgut Ozal, Turkey turned a deaf ear to Iraq's entreaties. In his own words, Ozal described Saddam to U.S. president George Bush in March 1990 as "the most dangerous man in the world." At least part of the reason for his concern with Saddam seems to have stemmed from a visit he paid to Tehran in early 1988. Baghdad disapproved of his trip and showed its displeasure by showering Tehran with missiles throughout the visit. Another likely source of Ozal's hatred of Saddam was a meeting held between Turkish prime minister Yildirim Akbulut and Saddam Husayn in Baghdad in May 1990. Having kept the Turkish prime minister waiting for a long time before he was received, Saddam launched into a nasty critique of Turkey's Euphrates water policy and then added, "What will happen to your country now? NATO has dispersed, it is no longer important. The U.S. will not help you. What will happen to you now?" Akbulut commented that Saddam's remark was not "very innocent." Echoing Ozal's sentiments, Akbulut stated plainly, "It would be good to put an end to the dictatorial rule of Saddam." And on another occasion, he said, "Iraq wants to establish superiority in the region. Its relations with Turkey have not been so sincere."[6]

Yet, starting soon after Ozal's death in 1993, Turkey increasingly warmed to Baghdad's seductive message. Even in early 1994, Turkey's official position remained that it supported the territorial integrity of Iraq but called upon Baghdad to "respect the UN resolutions, so that it could take its place again in the international community," and to "stop its steps against the population of northern Iraq."[7] Nevertheless, its actions increasingly belied these strong words. The first sign that Turkey was changing course was an influx of Turkish business delegations arriving in Baghdad in 1993 and 1994. These were private citizens from the Society of Businessmen and Industrialists, but the Iraqi media reported that they had delivered a political message in support of ending "the unjust blockade."[8] For the first time since 1990, a senior official—Foreign Under Secretary Ozdem Sanberk—arrived in Baghdad in April 1994 to discuss an agreement to empty and clean the Kirkuk–Dortyol oil pipeline. In Sanberk's words, because "Saddam is not likely to be overthrown soon," Turkey should engage in dialogue with the Iraqi regime.[9] As a further sign of Turkey's efforts to rebuild its ties to Iraq, beginning in 1994, many voices in the Turkish political arena began to demand an end to Operation Provide Comfort.

Yet, countervailing pressures prevented Ankara from tilting too far toward Baghdad. The Turkish government was reluctant to confront the

United States over Kurdistan, both in terms of U.S. diplomatic efforts to forge an anti-Saddam alliance and the maintenance of the northern no-fly zone. The Turkish army, for its part, favored the U.S. presence at Incirlik because it strengthened the ties between the two military establishments. Thus, beginning in 1994, the Turkish government adopted a middle course, agreeing to renew the mandate for Operation Provide Comfort, while simultaneously encouraging the Kurds to resume their dialogue with Saddam.[10] In the meantime, Turkey conducted raids into northern Iraq against the PKK to try to solve its own security problems. Whenever Turkish troops invaded Northern Iraq to try to stamp out PKK bases there, Iraq has made a point of protesting.[11]

The last major shift in Turkish–Iraqi relations occured under the premiership of Necmettin Erbakan, leader of the Islamist Refah (Welfare) party, who took office in late June 1996. Within a few weeks of taking power, Erbakan agreed to another five-month extension of Operation Provide Comfort, but he then sent the highest-level Turkish delegation to Baghdad since 1990. It was led by Justice Minister Sevket Kazan and National Education Minister Mehmet Saglam—the former being a member of Refah and Erbakan's close confidant—and discussed upgrading bilateral economic relations beyond the 1996 level of $200 million per year. During the visit, the Turks complained that their country was suffering as a result of the embargo, and for the first time ever they denounced it as "unjust." Furthermore, they promised to support the reimposition of Baghdad's rule over Iraqi Kurdistan.[12] Reportedly, the Turkish goal had been a trade agreement to the tune of $1 billion, which would go into effect after Resolution 986 was implemented.[13]

Behind this quantum leap in Turkey's pro-Iraq rhetoric lay not just the nature of the new Islamist government in Ankara, but also the fact that Iraq's acceptance of Resolution 986 meant Baghdad would soon have the ability to reward its friends with new economic deals, and Turkey did not want to be last in line for these rewards. Moreover, many Turkish politicians have come to believe that Saddam Husayn can and will neutralize the PKK once he is again in control of Kurdistan. Finally, one cannot discount the fear among some political circles in Turkey that the United States and—more so—Britain had hoped to establish a Kurdish state that will include southeastern Turkey. This notion has its roots in the 1920 Treaty of Sevres, in which the World War I allies promised to support the founding of a Kurdish political entity. Although most Turks have long since dismissed these suspicions, Turkish political and military involvement in Iraqi Kurdistan cannot be entirely divorced from this lingering fear, no matter how unwarranted.[14]

THE 1996 IRBIL CRISIS AND BEYOND

On August 31, 1996, Saddam's Republican Guards rolled into Irbil, smashing the PUK and Iraq National Congress (INC) forces defending the city. This assault was made possible by a deal struck between Baghdad and Barzani's KDP, which requested Iraqi support and then used the shock and confusion caused by the Republican Guard assault to drive Talabani's forces all the way to Sulaymaniyya. According to INC reports, once the Guard had secured its control over the city, Saddam's *mukhabarat* (intelligence service) moved in to arrest and execute PUK and INC supporters.[15] The occupation of Irbil and its environs also shattered a fairly large-scale U.S. covert action program in northern Iraq.

Iraq's attack on Irbil was a major event in the Turkish–Iraqi relationship. The crisis seemed to take Prime Minister Necmettin Erbakan by surprise, and he disappeared from the public's sight for several days.[16] Apparently, he was caught between his ideological anti-American line and the army's staunch pro-American position. Foreign Minister Tansu Çiller stepped in to fill the void and made two demands of the international community in return for Turkish cooperation: economic compensation for Turkey's losses caused by the embargo (which Turkish sources assessed at $27 billion from trade alone) and a temporary security zone in northern Iraq (to root out the PKK).[17] In addition, Çiller used the sudden evacuation of Operation Provide Comfort's military coordination commission (MCC) in Zakhu after the attack to demand changes in Operation Provide Comfort. The United States responded by reiterating its previous commitment that more than half of Iraqi oil exported under Resolution 986 would go through Turkey. This held the promise of adding some $250 million per year in transit fees to Turkey's coffers, in addition to the expected $1 billion in annual trade with Iraq that would be possible under the resolution. The United States also turned a blind eye to illicit oil shipments from Iraq to Turkey. The United States would not endorse the idea of a Turkish security zone, but it did not explicitly reject it.[18]

The course of events continued to push Ankara further into the Iraqi camp as the crisis unfolded. Not surprisingly, the Iraqi regime fiercely rejected the idea of a Turkish protectorate over part of Iraqi Kurdistan.[19]

Meanwhile, Turkey's Islamist circles attacked their prime minister for his passivity, and these two pressures may have combined to push Ankara into what increasingly began to look like a collision course with Washington. As early as September 11, Erbakan received an Iraqi diplomatic mission.[20] On September 19, Çiller disclosed that she had encouraged Saddam to reimpose his rule over the whole of Kurdistan and put an end to the PKK there. She was quick to add, "Otherwise, we will take [our own] measures."[21] (Later, Çiller would retract this statement, claiming she was misquoted.)

But when push came to shove and the Turkish military weighed in on the side of the United States, Turkey accepted the U.S. approach—albeit with some important modifications. Ankara agreed to serve as host for talks on November 15 between Barzani and Talabani under the auspices of the United States, Great Britain, and Turkey, which resulted in a partial reconciliation between the two Kurdish groups. The two warring sides agreed that a neutral force of non-Kurdish Iraqi minorities would serve as a peace monitoring force (PMF) that would demarcate and observe the cease-fire lines. Eventually, this constituted a force of 400 Iraqi Turkomans and Assyrians trained by Turkey and financed by the United States.[22] The agreement also established a supervisory peace monitoring group of representatives from the KDP, the PUK, the United States, Great Britain, and Turkey that would meet in Ankara.[23] Both sides even promised to exclude the PKK from their areas, although it was clear that this was merely a symbolic gesture. The Turkish parliament used the occasion of the flight from Iraq of the MCC to terminate Operation Provide Comfort on December 25, but the Turkish military then forced it to accept a new operation, Northern Watch, that continued essentially the same flight operations over the northern no-fly zone, under slightly modified guidelines.[24]

In May 1997 the military ousted the Erbakan government and replaced it with new secular coalition led by Mesut Yilmaz. This change in leadership generally institutionalized the pro-Western stance the military had previously imposed on the Erbakan government. Since then, Turkey's former pro-Iraqi rhetoric has largely evaporated, and Ankara has generally left diplomatic contacts to somewhat lower-profile officials. One of the most serious manifestations of Ankara's new determination to pursue its own interests, even at Baghdad's expense, was Turkey's intervention in northern Iraq during the summer of 1997. Between mid-May and the end of June, 10,000 Turkish troops invaded northern Iraqi Kurdistan and conducted large-scale counterinsurgency operations against the PKK. Barzani's KDP actively supported the Turks, and some Turkish troops remained inside Iraq even after the main force withdrew. Between June and September, Iraq strongly protested to the UN that there were no less than nineteen smaller-scale raids. On September 24, Turkey re-invaded, this time sending 15,000 troops backed by dozens of tanks. Iraq again protested vociferously, but it took no further action.[25] The situation deteriorated even further in October, when a Turkish cabinet minister told the Turkish newspaper *Hurriyet* that Turkey was creating a *cordon sanitaire* nine miles deep and staffed by 8,000 soldiers along its 198-mile border with Iraq.[26] In effect, although a full-fledged cordon has not actually been established, a Turkish presence inside Iraqi Kurdistan is now becoming a permanent feature of long stretches of the border.

Of course, neither relations with Baghdad nor pro-Iraqi statements have disappeared altogether, and the importance of the economic opportunities created by Resolution 986 has led Turkey to continue to expand its day-to-day relations with Iraq. In 1997, commerce between the two countries increased by 200 percent over the previous year. The frequency of Turkish business delegations also rose, and out of 700 contracts Baghdad signed under Resolution 986, at least 79 were with Turkey.[27] Diplomatic contacts similarly increased during 1997, and in September, Foreign Ministry Undersecretary Onur Oymen traveled to Baghdad, where he met with Izzat Ibrahim al-Duri, deputy chairman of the RCC and Tariq Aziz, deputy prime minister. The Oymen visit produced an agreement to increase the number of Turkish diplomats in Baghdad to seventeen.[28]

Indeed, what was most interesting about Turkish–Iraqi relations in the immediate aftermath of Erbakan's ouster was the apparent disconnect between politics and economics. At the political level, the Turks again support Kurdish reconciliation, continuation of Operation Northern Watch, and the maintenance of sanctions on Iraq until Baghdad is in full compliance with all UN resolutions. Moreover, Turkey has repeatedly flouted Iraqi sovereignty by conducting such lengthy counterinsurgency campaigns inside northern Iraq, ignoring Baghdad's constant protestations. Nevertheless, at the economic level, Turkey's relationship with Iraq flourishes. This demonstrates both countries' weakness: Ankara is desperate for the benefits its economy reaps from trade with Iraq, and Baghdad is desperate to cultivate relations with Turkey as a source of leverage to get the sanctions lifted altogether.

Thus, from Saddam's perspective, relations with Turkey over the last two years have been mixed. There is no doubt that Saddam believes he scored a series of important achievements in August and September 1996. He drove a wedge between the United States and the KDP by convincing Barzani to invite him to Irbil. He pushed Talabani into a strategic corner in Sulaymaniyya and forced the PUK to rely on Iran more heavily than before; yet, Saddam also forced Talabani to start negotiations with him. He smashed the U.S. intelligence-gathering and covert action base in Iraqi Kurdistan and forced the emergency evacuation of 6,480 Kurds and INC personnel to Turkey, Guam, and the United States.[29] The blow to the Central Intelligence Agency and the INC is a particularly important success for Saddam—this was the only Arab (non-Kurdish) opposition fighting him on Iraqi soil. Saddam also helped to push Ankara to end Operation Provide Comfort, which may prove to be the first step toward the reincorporation of Kurdistan into Saddam's Iraq. He saw the French pull out of Operation Northern Watch and the Turks impose new restrictions on U.S. and British air operations out of Incirlik that will make it harder for them to use Turkey as a base for airstrikes against Iraqi targets. Finally, the muted Turkish reaction to his attack on Irbil probably convinced him that Ankara will not oppose a bid to reimpose his rule over Iraqi Kurdistan, especially if in doing so he is able to extirpate the PKK.

On the other hand, Saddam also suffered some painful setbacks. The Turks failed to exert real diplomatic pressure on other members of the anti-Saddam coalition. Turkey also initiated a military relationship with Iraq's enemy, Israel, which has all the earmarks of a budding alliance. Iraq warned Turkey that it was "playing a dangerous game devised by the Zionist entity and the Americans,"[30] but the Turks were unimpressed. The Turkish decision to approve Operation Northern Watch was a major blow.[31] Saddam could not rely even on Erbakan's government—let alone its secular successor—to demand that the United States evacuate and allow him back into Kurdistan. Ultimately, Saddam was forced to admit that Turkey was not ready to trade its relationship with the United States for its relationship with Iraq.

Iraq's experience over the last few years suggests that Saddam has learned that Ankara will do little more than pay lip-service to his bid to return to Kurdistan. He can no longer expect even that much support from Turkey for ending the embargo. Turkey will continue to trade, but it is unlikely to exert diplomatic pressure on Iraq's behalf. Nor can Ankara be expected to challenge the United States by allowing Iraq to export oil through its pipeline beyond the amount authorized by the Security Council. Given that Erbakan was unwilling to break the embargo in such a blatant fashion, his secular successors certainly will not. As long as keeping Saddam out of Kurdistan remains a priority of the United States, Turkey will not actively oppose it and may continue to support the U.S. position by providing such aid as training and supplies for the peace monitoring force. Meanwhile, Ankara will continue to prevent PKK penetrations from northern Iraq into southeastern Turkey. Iraq can protest all it wants, but Turkey will continue its periodic invasions and probably will hold on to its new partial security zone there, although troop strength may fluctuate based on logistical and tactical considerations. Moreover, these positions are unlikely to change unless Ankara perceives a danger to its interests in Iraqi Kurdistan: Any hint that the Kurds are either moving toward independence from Iraq or sliding into chaos would trigger a sharp Turkish reaction. Turkey participated in the Ankara process to try to reconcile the warring Kurdish factions primarily so that it would be able to monitor and shape the U.S.–British–Kurdish dialogue. Ultimately, the Turks do not fully trust that their Western allies share their objectives for the Kurds, and therefore they are determined to keep a hand in the process.

There is little Saddam will be able to do about all of this. His greatest opportunity will be to reoccupy Kurdistan peacefully, invited by both parties, and perhaps even create a rift between Ankara and its American and British allies. Such an opportunity will present itself, for example, if and when the oil embargo is lifted. Now, under Resolutions 986 and 1153, the Kurdish zone is guaranteed 13 percent of Iraq's oil revenues. Once the embargo is off, Saddam will become the sole master of Iraqi oil revenues. Unless the Kurds then agree to return to his rule, no power will be able to force Saddam to share this wealth with them. Beyond this, Baghdad's options are limited. Iraq is unlikely to jeopardize the possibility of a more tangible improvement in Iraqi–Turkish relations by limiting commercial contacts with Turkey; it therefore has little economic leverage over Ankara. It is unlikely that Saddam would stop oil exports through the Iraqi–Turkish pipeline to protest Turkish policies. Baghdad might threaten to purchase food, textiles, and medicines elsewhere—thus denying Turkey this lucrative trade—but so far it has carefully refrained from such threats: Turkish goodwill is far too important for Saddam at this stage to risk over Kurdistan. Nor is he likely to try a military move against the Turks. The

Turkish army is tough, well-trained, armed with Western equipment—including more than 700 warplanes and 6,000 tanks—and Saddam has always shown great respect for Turkish strength. Even when Iraq's military power was at its height, except for May 1990, Saddam never threatened Turkey with force—either explicitly or implicitly—in the way that he has often threatened all of his other neighbors plus Israel. Indeed, whenever Iraq has had a dispute over Euphrates water, Saddam has blamed it on Syria, not Turkey. During the Gulf War, Iraqi attacks on Turkey were never more than rhetorical, and it is significant that he fired Scuds at Israel and Saudi Arabia but not Turkey—from which coalition warplanes were flying constant missions against Iraq. Given the deplorable state of Iraq's armed forces today, there is little reason to believe Saddam will suddenly decide he does have a military option against Ankara.

On the economic front, all Turkish governments have been unhappy about the repercussions of the embargo. Ankara sees the present arrangements that compensate Turkey somewhat for its losses as a result of the embargo as insufficient. As a result, Turkey continues the transport of oil across the Turkish–Iraqi border at Habur. Since Resolution 986 was implemented, this transport has become more difficult to justify. Apparently recognizing Turkey's losses since 1991 as a result of the embargo, the UN has been reluctant to intervene, but eventually this trade will have to be brought under the UN sanctions regime. Saddam, for his part, welcomes this trade because he too benefits from it. In September 1997 it was disclosed that the Turkish state-owned oil company, Petrol Offisi, would soon take over these semilegal oil imports.[32] At the same time, Turkey is canvasing Baghdad for a bigger share of Iraq's trade.[33] In exchange, Saddam expects Turkey to resume its Erbakan-style high-profile support for ending the embargo, thus complicating the U.S. diplomatic position. It is highly unlikely that, under the present secular government, Turkey will oblige, even though Saddam will be ready to pay a very high price for such renewed diplomatic support. A less obvious form of diplomatic assistance to Baghdad, however, is likely. Ankara behaves as if it perceives in Iraq a major opportunity but merely a small threat. Thus, if the United States and the UN take Turkey for granted and do not offer it more economic opportunities, Ankara is likely to step up its accommodation policy vis-à-vis Baghdad. The secular and pro-American government in Ankara notwithstanding, Kurdistan is where Turkey may draw closer to Iraq, thus helping to erode the American chokehold on Saddam's regime.

There are additional bones of contention between the two neighbors: Contrary to demands by the previous government that the embargo be terminated, at present Turkish spokesmen occasionally insist that, as a precondition for full Turkish–Iraqi cooperation, Iraq must fulfill all the resolutions of the Security Council.[34] Also, there is no agreement yet on water-sharing with Syria and Iraq: The Turks strongly object to the demand that the three parties share the water equally.[35]

NOTES

1 Many thanks to Alan Makovsky of the Washington Institute for Near East Policy for his insight on Turkish–Iraqi relations.

2 *Washington Post,* April 29, 1994. Jonathan C. Randal from Ankara, *Washington Post,* September 3, 1996.

3 *Voice of Iraqi People,* September 19, 1993, in *Foreign Broadcast Information Service–Near East and South Asia–Daily Report (FBIS-NES-DR),* September 24, 1993, p. 13.

4 See Safa' al-'Umar, Chairman of the Foreign Relations Committee of the Iraq National Congress, *Middle East News Agency (MENA),* June 7, 1995, in *FBIS-NES-DR,* June 7, 1995, p. 31.

5 See, for example,Tariq Aziz, *Iraqi News Agency (INA),* July 12, 1995, in *FBIS-NES-DR,* July 12, 1995, p. 36; see also *al-Thawra,* August 26, 1994.

6 Prime Minister Yeldirim Akbulut to *Ankara TRT TV Network,* December 20, 1990, in *FBIS–Western Europe (WEU)–DR TA2012191490,* December 21, 1990; *Anatolia News Agency,* Ankara, January 19, 1990, in *FBIS-WEU-DR TA1901164991,* January 22, 1990; *Reuters,* January 19, 1991.

7 See the declaration of the fourth foreign ministers meeting between Turkey, Iran, and Syria, on *Radio Damascus,* February 5, 1994, translated for a newsletter of the Israeli embassy, Washington, D.C., February 7, 1994, p. 4.

8 See, for example, *INA,* September 18, 1993, in *FBIS-NES-DR,* September 24, 1993, p. 13.

9 See *Washington Post,* April 29, 1994. There were 12,000 barrels in the pipeline, worth $120 million; two thirds of them belonged to Iraq, the rest to Turkey.

10 *Mideast Mirror,* June 16, 1994, quoting Turkish foreign ministry spokesman Ferhat Ataman.

11 See, for example, *al-Thawra,* attacking Turkish prime minister Tansu Çiller, as quoted by *INA,* July 12, 1995, in *FBIS-NES-DR,* July 12, 1995, p. 36. See

also denunciations by *INA,* April 8 and 9, 1995, in *FBIS-NES-DR,* April 10, 1995, pp. 32–33. See also in *INA* a particularly strong condemnation of the visit to Northern Iraq by Turkey's foreign minister and his team for talks with Barzani and Talabani. For reactions from the highest levels of Iraqi leadership to a statement by President Süleyman Demirel that Turkey should annex part of Iraq's territory, see *INA,* May 4, 1995, in *FBIS-NES-DR,* May 4, 1995, p. 37; May 5, 1995, p. 14.

12   *INA,* August 13, 1996, in *FBIS-NES-DR,* August 14, 1996, p. 21; see also Turkish minister of justice Sevket Kazan in Baghdad, *Ankara TRT TV,* August 13, 1996; *Anatolia* (Ankara), August 13, 1996, in *FBIS-NES-DR,* August 14, 1996, pp. 19–21.

13   *Wall Street Journal,* August 15, 1996.

14   For example, Deputy Prime Minister Bulent Ecevit remarked that "Britain has been the leading country causing chaos in the Middle East since World War I," while British Ambassador to Ankara David Logan was forced to deny Turkish charges that Britain favored breaking up Iraq and establishing a Kurdish state. Both comments in *Turkish Daily News,* February 13, 1998.

15   Based on interviews with INC members in London and Washington, D.C.

16   Erbakan's first coment was made on September 19, 1996. See *New Tork Times,* September 21, 1996.

17   Jonathan C. Randal from Ankara, *Washington Post,* September 3, 1996. *Reuters* from London, September 6, 1996. The Turks were thinking of a cordon between three and six miles wide; see *Reuters* from Ankara, September 6, 1996.

18   State Department Spokesman Glyn Davies, State Department Regular Briefing, Washington, D.C., September 5, 1996. See also *Reuters* from Washington, D.C., September 5, 1996; interview with Nuzhet Kandemir, the Turkish ambassador to the United States, *Washington Times,* September 10, 1996.

19   *INA,* September 9 and 10, 1996, in *FBIS-Serial JN0909172796, JN1009115396,* September 11, 1996.

20   *INA,* September 11, 1996, in *FBIS-Serial JN1109185796,* September 11, 1996.

21   *New York Times,* September 21, 1996.

22   *Clinton's Letter to Congress,* September 23, 1997, as reproduced by Washington Kurdish Institute, October 1, 1997. The force started its operations in mid-April 1997.

23   For the details of the agreement see *al-Mu'tamar,* November 8, 1996, p. 3; President Bill Clinton's letter to the Speaker of the House of Representatives and the President Pro Tempore of the Senate, *U.S. Newswire,* January 8, 1997.

24 *Agence France Presse (AFP),* December 25, 1996, in *FBIS-Serial NC2512205896,* December 25, 1996. For an angry Iraqi response see *INA,* December 26 1996, in *FBIS-Serial JN2612094396,* December 26, 1996. For the American position, see President Clinton's letter, *U.S. Newswire,* January 8, 1997. See also *al-Mu'tamar,* January 3, 1997, p. 3; *Turkish Daily News,* December 2, 1996, in *FBIS-Serial NC0212205496,* December 2, 1996; and *Turkiye,* December 4, 1996, in *FBIS-Serial NC0712145496,* December 7, 1996.

25 See both *AFP* and *Reuters,* September 24, 1997; *BBC,* September 26, 1997; *Reuters World Report,* September 25, 1997. For Foreign Minister Sahhaf complaining about nineteen raids, see *INA,* August 25, 1997, in *BBC Summary of World Broadcasts (BBC–SWB),* August 27, 1997.

26 *Associated Press (AP),* October 22, 1997, quoting *Hurriyet,* October 22, 1997.

27 *AFP,* September 21, 1997.

28 *Ankara TRT TV,* September 16, 1997, as quoted by *BBC–SWB,* September 19, 1987.

29 President Clinton's letter, *U.S. Newswire,* January 8, 1997.

30 See *al-Thawra,* September 4, 1997.

31 For angry reactions in Baghdad, see *al-Mu'tamar,* January 3, 1997, p. 3.

32 *Financial Times,* September 1, 1997, Europe edition; *Journal of Commerce,* September 3, 1997.

33 *Washington Kurdish Institute Mail Link,* September 15, 1997.

34 *Ankara TRT TV,* September 16, 1997, in *BBC–SWB,* September 19, 1997.

35 President Süleyman Demirel to *Ankara TRT TV,* September 16, 1997, in *BBC–SWB,* September 18, 1997.

Chapter 8

The Erstwhile Ally: Jordan

Over the last two decades, Jordan has been torn between Iraq and Israel. Too small and weak to pursue an independent course without a strong regional ally, it has oscillated between Jerusalem and Baghdad. During the Iran–Iraq War, King Hussein remained on very good terms with Israel, despite turning his country into one of Iraqi president Saddam Husayn's staunchest supporters and one of his main conduits to the outside world once the Iranian navy shut down Iraq's ports of Umm Qasr and Basrah. During much of the Gulf War, the king took a stance very favorable to Saddam, to a great extent because many Jordanians wholeheartedly cheered Saddam's occupation of Kuwait, a country and regime they disliked for the way Palestinians had been treated there. Palestinian Jordanians also perceived the occupation of Kuwait as a blow to Israel and a step toward pan-Arab action against it. As a number of Palestinians said at the time, they believed Kuwait would serve as a springboard for Saddam to compel the Gulf Arabs to commit their huge resources to the "liberation of Palestine." Nevertheless, before the Gulf War, King Hussein warned both Israel and Iraq not to be the first to use Jordan's air space against the other.[1] After the Gulf War, the king slowly distanced Jordan from Iraq. His pro-Iraqi stance had infuriated Saudi Arabia and Kuwait and placed a great strain on Jordan's relations with the United States, the only remaining superpower. Moreover, the Madrid process promised the opportunity finally to make peace with Israel. This dream became reality on October 26, 1994, when the king signed a peace treaty with Israeli prime minister Yitzhak Rabin. The peace treaty inaugurated a rapid warming of relations between Amman and Jerusalem and the equally rapid growth of a strategic partnership between the two countries.

Meanwhile, Iraq had much less to recommend itself anymore. Its army in ruins and its economy crippled by sanctions, Iraq could no longer offer Jordan political backing and military support—though it could still offer a limited market and an abundance of cheap oil. Relations remained cool but proper, even though the king's reservations vis-à-vis Saddam and his regime grew progressively more pronounced. Then, on April 15, 1994, King Hussein's personal friend, the Iraqi expatriate Shaykh Talib Suhayl al-Tamimi, was assassinated in Beirut by two Iraqi "diplomats."[2] Although in itself such an act could not determine Jordan's strategic agenda, it came at a time when the king seemed to be reassessing his relations with Iraq. The murder apparently tipped the scales in favor of drastically reducing Jordanian ties with Iraq in favor of building a closer relationship with Israel and the United States and repairing ties to the Gulf Cooperation Council (GCC). The deeper reasons for the change, however, were economic and geostrategic. Jordan needed new loans from the World Bank to repay its debts and needed favorable terms from the Paris and London clubs. Politically, the king was isolated and unable to play an active role in Middle Eastern politics.

Perhaps the clearest sign of the king's decision was his willingness to host Husayn Kamil when he defected, and his acerbic criticism of Saddam's regime afterwards. In an interview given to Israel's *Yediot Ahronot*, in itself an affront to Baghdad, the king declared, "If there is a change [in Iraq's leadership] this can only be a change for the better . . . I hope that this process promises the beginning of a new age—the beginning of a new life for the Iraqi people." The king criticized the "Iraqi leadership" for having started the Iran–Iraq War, for invading Kuwait, and for severely violating human rights, and he implied that, unlike Saddam Husayn, Husayn Kamil was ready for a rapprochement with Israel.[3] In a televised speech, the king denied that he had any ambitions in Iraq other than helping it out of its misery. Yet he reminded his audience that, until July 14, 1958, he himself was King Faysal II's heir as president of the [Iraqi–Jordanian] Arab Union. Iraq under Saddam Husayn, he pointed out, rejected his advice to withdraw from Kuwait, and by firing missiles at Israel over Jordanian air space, it put Jordan in grave jeopardy. In a very clear departure from previous Jordanian positions, the king also implied support for the U.S.–British position in the United Nations Security Council. Jordan, he disclosed, was also making emergency preparations to purchase oil from other sources, in case Iraq decided to stop selling oil to Jordan at favorable prices.[4] As part of a September 1995 trip to the United States, the king initiated a number of meetings in the United States and London with Iraqi expatriates, accompanied by Gen. (ret.) Mustafa Qaysi, former director of Jordan's General Intelligence, who was placed in charge of the "Iraqi file." Later he conducted telephone conversations with more Iraqi opposition leaders.[5] On February 5, 1996, the king appointed 'Abd al-Karim al-Kabariti as prime minister.[6] Unlike most of his colleagues, during the Gulf War Kabariti did not support Iraq. In his previous position as foreign minister, Kabariti was exceptionally critical of both Hafiz al-Asad's Syria and Saddam's Iraq, and he called for a change of regime in the latter.[7]

Amman also demonstrated its change of heart by enforcing the sanctions against Iraq. Whereas immediately after the Gulf War Jordan continued to serve as the primary conduit for smuggling into Iraq, the leaks have been gradually slowing since 1995. In December 1995, Jordan announced that its customs authorities had stopped "a few kilograms of extremely dangerous substances" destined for Iraq. Jordan also announced that in late November 1995 it had discovered Russian-made gyroscopes destined for Iraq—valued at $25 million. Saddam responded with a massive wave of arrests of some 700 Jordanian citizens, many of them for petty reasons.[8] Jordan was not deterred and in March 1996 it again confiscated illegal shipments destined to Iraq, this time missile and jet fighter parts.[9]

This policy continued in full force through the second half of 1996. In August, the king initiated a new crisis with Iraq when he blamed serious bread-riots in Karak in southern Jordan on "people [who] are known to be . . . either educated in Iraq or [to] have sympathies toward Iraq."[10] Prime Minister Kabariti accused the pro-Iraqi Ba'th party in Jordan of having been "very much involved in fomenting the riots,"[11] and a diplomatic crisis ensued.[12] Then, in November, a Jordanian driver was murdered in Iraq under suspicious circumstances, and the official Jordanian car he was driving vanished—with the diplomatic pouch he was carrying. Jordan's then–information minister, Marwan Muasher, leveled a verbal attack on Iraq, charging that the explanations given by the Iraqi authorities were not convincing.[13]

Jordan's decision to break with Iraq paid immediate dividends. The United States made clear in various ways that it would protect Jordan against Iraqi aggression.[14] In January 1996, Saudi foreign minister Prince Sa'ud al-Faysal visited Amman to discuss Iraq and to invite the king to visit Riyadh.[15] A few days after Kabariti was sworn in, the king and his new prime minister performed the "little pilgrimage" (*'umra*) in Mecca and met in Riyadh with Crown Prince 'Abd Allah.[16] Although King Hussein probably was disappointed that he did not get an audience with King Fahd himself, the meeting with 'Abd Allah opened the way for increased Jordanian exports to Saudi Arabia—during the first six months of 1996 they more than doubled.[17] It also led to a Saudi announcement that the kingdom was ready to resume oil exports to Jordan.[18] The following August, King Hussein got his audience with King Fahd. Their meeting produced new agreements that further boosted economic cooperation and began a dialogue on ways to enhance cooperation over security.[19]

Nevertheless, Jordan's ties to Iraq were too extensive to be severed completely, despite heavy pressure from Riyadh and Washington. In particular, Jordan has continued to rely on Iraq as a source of cheap oil and an easy market. Saddam could not have been pleased by the various insults he had suffered from King Hussein, but he would not stop the flow of subsidized oil to Jordan or the flow of goods from Jordan to markets in Iraq—Jordan has been Iraq's only outlet to the world and its main source of hard currency. In different ways, the relationship was kept alive. Remarkably, one day after the defection of Husayn Kamil the Iraqi media extolled a cable sent by the king to Saddam, congratulating him on the occasion of the Prophet's birthday.[20] Likewise, in the midst of the crisis, the Iraqi president sent a cable congratulating King Hussein on the occasion of his coronation anniversary.[21] A few days later the king replied in a cable, although the message was not particularly warm.[22] Following the rioting in Karak and the accusations against Iraq from the king and Kabariti, two Jordanian cabinet ministers assured the *Jordan Times* that the Jordanian Ba'th party was the guilty party, not the Iraqi regime, and that therefore trade relations would not be affected.[23] Finally, in November 1996, the king was visited by Iraqi vice president Taha Muhyi al-Din Ma'ruf and then–Foreign Minister Muhammad Sa'id al-Sahhaf. No joint communiqués were issued, but the meetings were the message.[24]

A key influence on Amman's foreign policy is the tremendous sentiment among the Jordanian people in favor of Iraq. Many in Jordan, especially among fundamentalist circles, support Saddam Husayn because of his anti-American and anti-Israeli positions. Pan-Arab intellectuals and many journalists also identify with the Iraqi leader. Some reporters had received expensive gifts from Saddam during the height of Iraqi–Jordanian cooperation. Others, even though they may recognize his poor judgment in political decisions (as opposed to his abuse of human rights), see him as a proud Arab who stands up to Israel and the United States. Their support for him was particularly strong during the Gulf War, but it outlived the war.[25] Moreover, even those secular intellectuals and government officials who generally have little sympathy for Saddam resent the hardships that the international embargo has inflicted on the Iraqi people. In private conversations, such people complain that implementing United Nations Security Council Resolution 986 is insufficient to alleviate the suffering of the Iraqi people, and only the lifting of the embargo altogether will be sufficient. That this would greatly strengthen Saddam Husayn and enable him to return to his previous policies is not an important consideration in their thinking.

As powerful as ideology and sentiment is in drawing Jordan toward Iraq, Iraqi–Jordanian economic ties are probably more important. In the mid-1990s, Iraq supplied Jordan with 60,000 to 70,000 barrels per day (bpd) of oil and oil derivatives; 50 percent of this oil was provided to Jordan at no cost.[26] For 1997, the two sides signed an agreement fixing the price of a barrel of oil at $19.10. The total quantity sold to Jordan would also rise by 7 percent more than the 1996 level, to 68,500-69,000 bpd of crude and 19,000-19,180 bpd of oil derivatives. This means that in 1997 Jordan received Iraqi oil worth $625 million, for which it paid $325 million. Moreover, this cost was covered by a new $255 million trade protocol on Jordan's exports to Iraq, and the other $70 million was written-off as partial payment for Iraq's debt to Jordan.[27] In 1998, the two countries agreed that Iraq would increase Iraqi oil sales to Iraq beyond the 1997 amount. Iraq agreed to supply 4.8 million metric tons annually (around 96,000 bpd), 50 percent of which at no cost, and of the remaining cost to Jordan, Iraq agreed to deduct $300 million as repayment of its debt to Jordan.[28] In other words, Iraqi oil sales to Jordan have been increasing annually: In 1992, 7.7 percent of Jordan's total domestic exports went to Iraq; in 1993, it was 11.2 percent; in 1994, 13.3 percent; and in 1995, the figure rose to 19.0 percent. Likewise, Iraq has purchased more Jordanian exports; Iraq's share of Jordanian exports to Arab countries increased between 1992 and 1995 from 21.8 to 42.0 percent,[29] despite the fluctuations in the two countries' political relationship.

Jordanian industry is particularly dependent on Iraq. Jordan has always exported more basic commodities than luxury consumer goods, and despite the sanctions, the Iraqi market can still afford many of these products. Since it resumed oil sales under Resolution 986, Iraq's buying power has increased substantially. Official figures are unavailable, but pro-Iraqi industrial circles in Jordan claim that Iraq absorbs 30 percent of Jordan's total industrial products, and that 40,000 Jordanian jobs depend on economic ties with Iraq.[30] In 1996, Jordan's registered domestic workforce was roughly 342,000, whereas its total domestic workforce (excluding non-Jordanians) was assessed at 865,000.[31] Consequently, some 11.7 percent of Jordan's registered and 4.6 percent of its total domestic workforce depended on trade with Iraq. With Jordan's official unemployment rate continuing to hover around 30 percent, Amman cannot afford to lose the Iraqi market.

Finally, one cannot forget Iraq's debt to Jordan as a binding force. In 1989, Iraq owed Jordan roughly $800 million, but by March 1996, the figure had reached almost $1.3 billion.[32] The Iraqi debt represents more than 25 percent of Jordan's total national debt. Even if Saudi Arabia and Kuwait were to agree to provide Jordan with cheap oil to replace Iraq's (and so far, it is clear that neither is considering such subsidized sales to Jordan[33]), they are not willing to cover Iraq's debt to Jordan nor can they realistically replace Iraq as a market for Jordanian exports. Saudi imports from Jordan for the first six months of 1996 were no more than $54 million, and this was twice what it had been in the last half of 1995. The taste, habits, and purchasing power of consumers in the GCC states are quite different from those of the Iraqis. The Gulf Arabs are accustomed to expensive, high-quality Western, Japanese, and South Korean commodities, not those which Jordan can produce. Thus, Jordan's exports to Saudi Arabia in 1995 consisted mainly of live animals, vegetables, and some pharmaceutical products.[34] Also, unlike Saudi Arabia, Iraq does not levy customs duties on Jordanian industrial products.[35] Under these circumstances, it is no wonder that the Jordanian prime minister had to assure his business community that any improvement in Jordanian–Saudi relations would not come at the expense of economic ties with Iraq.[36]

These powerful connections began to pull Jordan back toward Baghdad after the king began to see a number of problems with Amman's anti-Iraq stance. Initially, the king had apparently persuaded himself that the defection of Husayn Kamil and Jordan's switch to the anti-Iraq camp would galvanize the Iraqi opposition and its supporters—most notably the United States—leading to a rapid ouster of Saddam. Yet, none of this materialized—Husayn Kamil, too, proved ineffective, and even a burden. Moreover, the Saudis made important strides toward reconciliation, but relations remained cool, and Kuwait would not even go that far. Consequently, Jordan's economic and diplomatic situations improved, but not in the radical fashion Amman had envisioned.

Jordan's position in September 1996 during the U.S.–Iraqi confrontation over Irbil was among the first indications that the Jordanian pendulum was on its way back. Jordan backed away from its tough anti-Baghdad position, rejecting Washington's request to stage warplanes from Jordanian bases against Iraq. Crown Prince Hassan Bin Talal described the U.S. cruise missile attack, which eventually formed part of the U.S. response, as "a blunt instrument without a clear policy," and implied that he supported an end to the embargo.[37] More than anything else, the prince's position was that of exasperation at what he saw as "haphazard" U.S. policy toward Iraq. The United States, he complained, could not decide whether its goal was to rehabilitate Saddam or depose him.[38] Echoing Jordanian popular sentiment, the Jordanian press was downright hostile to the U.S. missile attack.[39]

In early 1997, it became clear that Amman had concluded that its activities against Saddam's regime had not proven fruitful, and that it was moving back toward its previous support for Iraq. In February 1997, the king called Saddam for the first time since the August 1995 defection of the Kamils, to congratulate him on the Muslim holiday of 'Id al-Fitr.[40] On March 19, 1997, Kabariti was removed as prime minister and was replaced by 'Abd al-Salam al-Majali. Unlike Kabariti, Majali enjoys excellent relations with Saddam and his regime, and this move was immediately interpreted around the world as a sign that the king wanted to repair his relationship with Saddam. Majali lost no time; three days after his appointment as prime minister, he met with Iraqi deputy prime minister Tariq 'Aziz. The latter congratulated him on his new job and declared that, despite a recent attempt to "create tension," relations between the two countries and leaderships were "close"; Iraq wanted to expand mutual economic relations; and Aqaba would continue to serve as "one of Iraq's main outlets." In turn, the new prime minister declared that his country was determined to enhance mutual relations, and that he hoped to see a quick end to the suffering of the Iraqi people. Crown Prince Hassan also met with 'Aziz— a diplomatic gesture of the first order.[41] Finally, on that same eventful day, the UN approved twenty-two new Jordanian–Iraqi agreements for supplying Iraq with Jordanian detergents worth $26 million and announced that a deal worth an additional $120 million (for cooking oil and medicines) was at an advanced stage of negotiations in the UN.[42]

Since this series of meetings, Jordan has continued to reforge its ties to Saddam's Iraq. In an interview to *al-Hayat* in April 1997, Majali criticized U.S. secretary of state Madeleine Albright's call to topple Saddam, pointing out that this will only strengthen the Iraqi leader.[43] Following the failure of the military coup d'état in the summer of 1996, the king abandoned his plan to turn Amman into a center of opposition activity centered around the *Wifaq*. Although it was allowed to stay and operate, the Wifaq was forced to lower its media profile.[44] According to reliable reports, beginning in January 1997 many Iraqi dissidents started leaving Jordan in response to Jordanian warnings that their safety was no longer guaranteed.[45] As reported by a staunch pro-Iraqi (although not always accurate) source, a Jordanian official confirmed that Jordan will no longer have political ties with the Iraqi opposition, that it would not be committed to their "political protection," and that it does not seek a change of regime in Baghdad.[46]

As could only be expected, Iraq is doing everything in its power to draw Jordan back into close bilateral relations. Baghdad's tactics have taken the form of Saddam's usual combination of *al-tarhib wal-targhib* (intimidation and enticement). On the one hand the Iraqis have warned Jordan against any attempt to tear itself from the Iraqi embrace. The murder in late 1995 and early 1996 of five Jordanian students enrolled at Iraqi universities was a typical Iraqi method of sending a diplomatic message.[47] Another such warning came in the form of an angry Iraqi protest against the king's accusation that Iraq instigated the Karak bread riots of August 1996.[48] Iraqi radio implied that, if the king continued his slander campaign, Iraq might really begin to interfere in Jordanian domestic politics.[49] On the other hand, Iraq is simultaneously trying to charm the Jordanian business community by importing Jordanian industrial products duty-free.[50] Iraqi officials have also promised preferential treatment for Jordanian tenders, and in June 1996 senior cabinet ministers told a Jordanian delegation that, although imports through Umm Qasr and Basra will be cheaper once Resolution 986 is fully implemented, Iraq will "not exclude Aqaba."[51] Most important, Iraq holds over Jordan's head the oil supplies "Sword of Damocles": Even though it has never threatened explicitly to end exports to Jordan, the mere possibility that oil shipments could end is so alarming that Amman must avoid a complete rupture with Baghdad at almost all cost.

As long as it has no alternative to Iraq as an economic partner, Amman will continue its close cooperation with Baghdad and may even seek to enhance it. This cooperation provides Iraq with several important benefits. Jordan is a large trading partner that Iraq could use to violate the international embargo. The new revenues Iraq has gained from Resolution 986 will enable Saddam to divert his unsupervised assets—mainly revenues from oil sales to Jordan and Turkey, plus oil smuggled through Iranian territorial waters—toward the rebuilding of his military machine. Jordan plays a role here too: If Jordan once again turns a blind eye to illicit Iraqi imports of military technology through its territory, this will further erode UNSCOM's efforts to dismantle Saddam's WMD arsenal. In addition, Iraq's cozy relations with Jordan provide Baghdad with an easy outlet for the world travel of wealthy Iraqis and Saddam's officials. The only other outlets—Turkey and Syria—are arduous and politically problematic.

Thus, Saddam Husayn's nightmare is a Jordanian–Saudi–Kuwaiti agreement that would provide Jordan with cheap oil and help Jordan's industrialists to adapt to new markets in the Gulf, the West Bank and Gaza, and even Israel. But without a new and very generous attitude toward Jordan on the part of the Saudis and the Kuwaitis, Saddam has little to fear on this front. And at present, neither Saudi Arabia nor Kuwait has provided any indication that they are seriously contemplating such an attitude.

Even if no change occurs in the positions of Saudi Arabia and Kuwait, the United States and the UN could make certain demands of Jordan. One realistic demand should be to continue to expose illegal Iraqi imports. Jordan can also shut down any Iraqi-owned commercial establishments in Amman that is caught smuggling weapons parts or other military technology to Iraq, as well as illicit luxury imports for Iraq's elite. Of greatest importance, the Saudis and the Kuwaitis must be convinced that, unless they are ready to change their attitude in a very profound fashion, Jordan—Iraq's most important contact-point with the outside world—will be lost as a strategic asset in the struggle to change the regime in Baghdad.

NOTES

1   Based on interviews with well-informed Israeli and Western sources who preferred to remain anonymous.

2   The assassination resulted in Lebanon breaking diplomatic relations with Iraq. See, for example, *al-Sharq al-Awsat,* April 16, 1994; *Jordan Times,* April 23, 1994.

3   The king's interview with Smadar Peri, *Yedi'ot Ahronot,* August 14, 1995, pp. 1, 5.

4   *Jordan TV,* August 23, 1995, in *Foreign Broadcast Information Service– Near East and South Asia–Daily Report (FBIS-NES-DR),* August 24, 1995, pp. 43–47.

5   These opposition leaders included Ahmad Chalabi, secretary of the liberal Iraq National Congress; Shaykh Muhammad Bahr al-'Ulum, a Shi'i *mujtahid* close to the congress; Dr. Iyad 'Alawi, secretary; Salah al-Shaykhali, Dr. Tahsin Mu'alla, and Colonels Tufiq al-Yasiri and 'Adnan Nuri of the Wifaq; and Muhammad Baqir al-Hakim, leader of the Tehran-based Supreme Assembly of the Islamic Revolution in Iraq (SAIRI). The king also sent communications to Jalal Talabani and Mas'ud Barzani. Information based on author's interview with a leading figure in the Iraqi opposition, London, late 1995.

6   *Amman Jordan TV Network,* February 4, 1996, in *FBIS-NES-DR,* February 5, 1996, p. 37.

7   Lamis Andoni, in *Jordan Times,* February 5, 1996.

8   *Ha'aretz,* December 27, 1995, quoting various news agencies, p. A11.

9   See, for example, *Ha'aretz,* March 8, 1996.

10 *Mideast Mirror,* August 19, 1996, p. 15.

11 *Washington Post,* August 20, 1996.

12 *Baghdad Mother of Battles Radio,* August 23, 1996, in *FBIS-DR-NES,* August 23, 1996; *Agence France Presse (AFP),* August 23, 1996.

13 *al-Mu'tamar,* November 22, 1996.

14 *Amman Jordan TV Network,* January 7, 1996; *Jordan Times,* January 8, 1996, in *FBIS-NES-DR,* January 11, 1996, pp. 49–52.

15 *al-Hayat,* January 11, 1996.

16 *Reuters,* February 11, 1996.

17 *Jordan Times,* August 14, 1996.

18 Foreign Minister Prince Sa'ud al-Faysal, quoted in *Middle East Economic Survey (MEES),* January 22, 1996.

19 *Jordan Times,* August 14, 1996.

20 *INA,* August 9, 1995, in *FBIS-NES-DR,* August 10, 1995, p. 28.

21 *INA,* August 11, 1995, in *FBIS-NES-DR,* August 11, 1995, p. 19.

22 *INA*, August 17, 1995, in *FBIS-NES-DR*, August 18, 1995, p. 28.

23 Those predicting business as usual were Trade and Industry minister 'Ali Abu al-Raghib and Transport minister Nasir al-Lawzi, *Jordan Times*, August 21, 1996.

24 *al-Mu'tamar*, November 15 and December 13, 1996; *Los Angeles Times*, December 20, 1996.

25 For examples of contemporary support for Saddam, see the speech of 'Abd Allah al-'Akaylah, the head of the Jordanian Islamic Action Front (IAF) delegation in Baghdad, upon their meeting with Tariq 'Aziz, *INA*, April 23, 1994, in *FBIS-NES-DR*, April 25, 1994, pp. 43–44; and both the lavish praise to Saddam Husayn and the "agreement" signed between the Iraqi Ba'th and the IAF, *INA*, April 23 and 26, 1994, in *FBIS-NES-DR*, April 26, 1994, p. 23.

26 See, for example, *Jordan Times*, January 26, 1994. See also *Shihan*, January 20–26, 1996, pp. 13, 31, in *FBIS-NES-DR*, January 24, 1996, p. 28; *Jordan Times*, January 20, 1997; and an economic "responsible source" in Jordan confirming this fact, *al-Majd*, January 22, 1996. See also Samih Darwaza, Jordan's minister of energy, confirming that his country was receiving 60,000 to 70,000 barrels per day "on soft conditions": *INA*, August 18, 1996, in *FBIS-NES-DR*, August 18, 1996.

27 Computed from *Jordan Times*, January 20, 1997; see also *MEES*, January 27, 1997.

28 See *Jordan Times*, January 2, 1998.

29 Computing from the Hashemite Kingdom of Jordan, *Statistical Yearbook 1995*, no. 46, (Amman: Department of Statistics, October 1996), pp. 460–461, tables 19/1/1, 19/1/2. See also International Monetary Fund, *Directions of Trade Statistics Yearbook* (Washington, D.C.: IMF Publications Service, 1995), p. 271. (JD1=$1.3)

30 *Mideast Mirror*, September 25, 1996, p. 14; *Washington Post*, September 21, 1996.

31 Jordan, *Statistical Yearbook 1995*, p. 51, Table 4/1/1; the information contained therein is for 1994. The annual increase rate was assessd at just over 3 percent; Minister of Labour and Social Affairs Nader Abu Sha'er to *Jordan Times*, November 28, 1995.

32 Dr. Ziad Fariz, governor of Jordan's central bank, to *Jordan Times*, March 18, 1996. See also *Jordan Times*, May 30, 1996 reporting $1.3 billion; and Trade minister 'Ali abu al-Raghib, *al-Ra'y*, January 24, 1996, reporting $1.2 billion.

33 A senior Jordanian official disclosed that the Saudis were ready to step in, but

the oil "will definitely be at a higher cost"; *Jordan Times,* August 21, 1996.

34 *Jordan Times,* March 28–29, 1996; Jordan's central bank governor to *al-Aswaq,* March 17, 1996, in *FBIS -NES-DR,* March 18, 1996, p. 55.

35 Jordan's central bank governor to *al-Aswaq,* March 17, 1996. The Jordanian national debt in March 1996 was $4.465 billion. Jordan's exports to Iraq are mainly vegetable oil (much of it coming from the far East and repackaged in Jordan) and canned foods, medicines, pesticides, textiles, and paper and printed matters. Jordan also sells tires to Iraq, most of which are reexport. For the trade and services agreement with Saudi Arabia, see *al-Ra'y,* August 14, 1996, in *FBIS-NES-DR,* August 19, 1996; for comments of Jordanian industrialists to *al-Ra'y,* as reported in *Iraqi TV Network,* August 30, 1996, see *FBIS-NES-DR,* August 30, 1996.

36 *INA,* August 18, 1996, in *FBIS-NES-DR,* August 18, 1996.

37 *Washington Post,* September 21, 1996.

38 *Jordan Times,* September 11, 1996, in *FBIS-Serial JN1109111396,* September 11, 1996.

39 See report in *Jordan Times,* September 7, 1996.

40 *Kol Yisrael,* 1800 News, February 8, 1997.

41 *Jordanian News Agency* from Amman, March 22, 1997.

42 *French News Agency,* March 22, 1997.

43 *Ha'aretz,* April 14, 1997.

44 See, for example, the report by *al-Sharq al-Awsat,* October 6, 1997, in *BBC Summary of World Broadcasts (BBC–SWB),* October 8, 1997.

45 *Radio Monte Carlo,* January 24, 1997.

46 See *al-Quds al-'Arabi,* January 28, 1997.

47 See *al-Hadath,* April 22, 1996; *Jordan Times,* May 30, 1996. *al-Hadath* reported also an Iraqi plot to assassinate Prime Minister 'Abd al-Karim al-Kabariti. No further confirmation could be obtained, but the March 1996 expulsion from Amman of Hussein Faraj, Iraq's assistant press attaché, may be connected with this plot; see the news agencies, March 25, 1996, as reported in *al-Malaff al-'Iraqi,* no. 52 (April 1996), p. 56. According to *al-Sharq al-Awsat,* April 14, 1996, Jordan also ordered Nuri al-Wayyis, Iraq's ambassador to Jordan, not to return from leave, owing to too much involvement in Jordanian affairs.

48 In Jordan, at a parliamentary session, the king accused forces "outside of the country" of instigating the August 1996 *fitna* (civil anarchy); see *al-Hayat,*

August 23, 1996. In protest, Jordan expelled Iraqi press attaché 'Adil Ibrahim and refused to allow Khalid Muslih to take up his position as first secretary at the Iraqi embassy; see *AFP,* August 23, 1996, in *FBIS-Serial NC2308143196,* August 23, 1996. The secretary general of Jordan's pro-Iraqi Ba'th party, Taysir al-Humsi, and a few other senior members of the party were arrested; see *Reuters* from Amman, August 22 and September 10, 1996).

49 *Mother of Battle Radio,* August 20, 1996, in *FBIS-NES-DR,* August 20, 1996.

50 Jordan's central bank governor to *al-Aswaq,* March 17, 1996, in *FBIS-NES-DR,* March 18, 1996, p. 55. Jordan's exports to Iraq are mainly vegetable oil (much of it coming from the far East and repacked in Jordan) and canned foods, medicines, pesticides, textiles and paper and printed matters. Jordan also sells tyres to Iraq, much of which is reexport. For the trade and services agreement with Saudi Arabia, see *al-Ra'y,* August 14, 1996, in *FBIS-NES-DR,* August 19, 1996; for the comments of Jordanian industrialists to *al-Ra'y,* reported in *Iraqi TV Network* on August 30, 1996, see *FBIS-NES-DR,* August 30, 1996.

51 *Jordan Times,* August 3, 1996; see also *al-Aswaq,* June 20, 1996, in *FBIS-NES-DR,* June 24, 1996, p. 40.

Chapter 9

Iraq's Relations with the Arabian Peninsula

O ther than Iraq, the two states most intimately involved in the crisis of 1990–1991 were Kuwait and Saudi Arabia. These are also the states that remain most staunchly opposed to any leniency toward Saddam Husayn and his regime in Baghdad. Likewise, they are the targets of Baghdad's harshest political attacks and media assaults. Saddam has tried to intimidate both into political submission and, occasionally, his regime has tried to entice the Saudis into cooperation, but so far to no avail. All the same, certain differences have evolved between the positions of these two states toward Baghdad.

KUWAIT

In October 1994, Iraq officially recognized Kuwait's sovereignty for the second time in its history. The first time was in October 1963, when the first Iraqi Ba'th regime recognized Kuwait in return for a generous subsidy. Baghdad's more recent acknowledgement of Kuwaiti sovereignty is seen as legally binding by the international community, but not necessarily by the the Iraqi regime itself. On each anniversary of the invasion (*Yawm al-Nida*, the "Day of the Call," in Iraqi parlance), the Iraqi media and leadership reemphasize the legitimacy—indeed, the unavoidable necessity—of the attack on Kuwait on August 2, 1990. In Baghdad's mythology, the al-Nida offensive was a clear-cut case of self-defense. The Iraqis still regularly warn Kuwait that it is continuing to provoke Iraq and will suffer the consequences.[1] For example, the editor of Iraq's *al-Jumhuriyya*, Salah

Mukhtar, wrote in 1994 on the anniversary of the invasion:

> When Iraq took the giant historic step of entering Kuwait on August 2, 1990, few international and regional quarters thought that this exceptionally significant and serious move would trigger a series of . . . events . . . that would help mankind avert a bleak future conceived under a horrible U.S. scheme to control the world . . . . The U.S. wanted Iraqi territory to be the battlefield, but the entry into Kuwait has changed that, for Kuwaiti territory became the battlefield . . . . The U.S. wanted to enslave world peoples and plunder their resources . . . thus Iraq has served mankind [by invading Kuwait] . . . [A]s we relive the events of that historic day . . . [we tell the United States and its collaborators] that their anti-Iraq policies are sheer folly.[2]

So far, no Iraqi spokesman has officially declared the October 1994 border recognition null and void, but an announcement by Iraqi vice president Taha Yasin Ramadan implied delegitimization.[3]

Furthermore, there is every reason to believe that when the first opportunity presents itself, the Ba'th regime will again conquer Kuwait and annex it. Certainly many ordinary Iraqis believe this to be the case. Yet, the regime itself has been very careful never to articulate such an aim publicly. Moreover, at least since their scare in October 1994, the Iraqis have taken the opposite approach. Today, while it fully justifies its occupation of Kuwait in 1990–1991, Baghdad also calls for a rapprochement with Kuwait.

If Iraq could achieve such a rapprochement, it would eliminate the staunchest opposition in the Arab world to Iraq's rehabilitation. If Kuwait were to normalize relations with Iraq, exchange diplomatic missions, and resume full economic relations, Iraq would very quickly resume its standing in the Arab league, and Iraqi president Saddam Husayn would again be invited to Arab summits—something he has been denied since 1990. Normalizing relations with Kuwait could also pull the carpet out from under Washington's military containment of Iraq, because Iraq would undoubtedly press Kuwait to evict U.S. forces from Kuwaiti soil. Under such circumstances it would be very difficult for Saudi Arabia to allow U.S. air patrols over southern Iraq to fly from Saudi territory.

Yet, there is little risk of such a scenario. The critical obstacle to any reconciliation between Iraq and Kuwait is Saddam Husayn's continued rule in Baghdad. As long as Saddam is the head of state in Iraq, it is inconceivable that Baghdad could admit that the occupation of Kuwait was a mistake or an illegal act, because this would imply that Saddam was an international criminal or, worse still, a fool. Saddam can never allow any major decision of his to be portrayed as a mistake because it would call into question his legitimacy as ruler of Iraq. Yet Kuwait will require just such a clear statement of Iraqi contrition as a precondition for improved relations. Remarkably, Saddam still seems to believe that if he can just intimidate the little desert emirate enough, it will eventually agree to normalization, despite Baghdad's scathing rhetoric.

The persistence of Iraq's bullying is one of the principal factors reinforcing Kuwait's determination to keep Iraq contained. Of all the Arab states, Kuwait most staunchly demands that Iraq fulfill *all* of the UN requirements before it can be reintroduced into the Arab fold and the international community. Of course, Kuwait also has the greatest stake in the other terms of the ceasefire agreement beyond Iraq's forced disarmament. Three of the other conditions of the ceasefire were that Iraq renounce its claims to Kuwait, return the roughly 600 Kuwaiti citizens whom Iraqi forces arrested and took to Baghdad during the occupation, and return the Kuwaiti military equipment and other property Iraq seized after the invasion.

Kuwait has made no secret of its hatred of Saddam. Kuwaiti politicians have openly called for a change of regime in Baghdad, warning that the present regime will endanger the entire gulf region.[4] Of all the regional states, only Kuwait fully supported the U.S. military operation in September 1996. Yet, the Kuwaiti government is not entirely unanimous on its Iraq policy, and at times this leads to mixed signals from Iraq's most resolute Arab opponent. Some Kuwaiti leaders seem to believe that Saddam is "the devil we know" and that the United States will remain in the Gulf only to keep Saddam boxed-in. Once he is toppled, Kuwait will be exposed to his successor. Thus, in February 1996, Minister of Information Shaykh Sa'ud Nasir al-Sabah argued that Kuwait should prefer

> an enemy you know and not an enemy you do not know. We know Saddam, . . . and the world knows that Saddam is an enemy . . . of the world, not just that of Kuwait . . . but he remains a weak enemy, which is better than . . . a regime we do not know." Kuwait, he added, is worried lest "the international sympathy with us [will end] when Saddam is gone, while the existing problems are not solved.[5]

Although Kuwait has fiercely defended the containment of Iraq since the

Gulf War, it has only recently begun to try to support this position actively with diplomatic and economic overtures in the region. Within the last year, Kuwait has grudgingly made a number of gestures toward Jordan, Sudan, and Yemen, each of which had sided with Iraq during the Gulf War. In July 1997, Kuwaiti Airways resumed its flights to Amman, a Sudanese minister of state visited Kuwait, and Kuwaiti academics were permitted to visit Yemen.[6]

Kuwait began to receive some war reparations as a result of Iraqi oil sales under UN Security Council Resolution 986. Yet, the negotiations concerning the 600 missing Kuwaitis have gone nowhere.[7] The Iraqis claim that the missing Kuwaitis "disappeared" during the Shi'i *intifada* (uprising) in March 1991. Whether true or not—and it seems highly dubious—this response strongly suggests that Kuwait will never see these people again. Even if they are still alive in Iraqi jail cells, which some of them may be, Saddam's regime cannot afford to admit that it was lying all of these years by producing the missing people. Such an admission would further undermine its efforts to have the UN sanctions lifted. Likewise, there is no sign that Iraq will return Kuwait's stolen war materiel any time soon. Indeed, most of this equipment continues to be employed by Iraqi military units.

For these reasons, but mostly because the man who ordered the invasion of Kuwait is still in power in Baghdad, a Kuwaiti–Iraqi rapprochement is not in the offing. Kuwait will continue to struggle against any leniency toward Iraq, while Iraq's anger at Kuwait will only increase over time. For the same reason, Kuwait has no choice but to move forward in its relations with other Arab states who backed Saddam during the Gulf War. Kuwait must seek a true reconciliation with Jordan, and it ought to develop a useful dialogue with the more moderate elements in the Iraqi opposition.[8] The sooner the Kuwaiti leadership internalizes this conclusion, the more difficult it will be for Saddam Husayn to break out of his isolation.

SAUDI ARABIA

Since the Gulf War, Iraq's goal in its foreign policy toward Saudi Arabia has been to induce the kingdom to leave the animosities of the war behind and look forward to a new era of cooperation. Iraqi diplomatic and political efforts are aimed at securing Saudi neutrality, if not renewed amity with Baghdad. Iraq's minimal goal with Saudi Arabia is to try to convince Riyadh not to block Baghdad's reintegration into the mainstream of Arab politics. Beyond this, Iraq hopes that Riyadh will agree to full normalization and will push to have the Iraqi regime reinstated in the Arab League. Baghdad's best-case scenario would also see Riyadh evict U.S. troops stationed in Saudi Arabia, or at least prohibit the United States from using the kingdom as a base for U.S. missions over Iraq—either overflights in southern Iraq to enforce the no-fly zone, or combat missions as part of an U.S. air campaign against Iraq. Finally, Iraq would like to see Saudi Arabia raise its voice in favor of an end to the UN oil embargo. This does not mean that the Iraqi regime has forgotten, let alone forgiven, Saudi support for the allied forces during and after the Gulf War. Indeed, if and when Saddam's Iraq returns to the Arab fold and rebuilds its military power, Saddam Husayn may be counted on to seek revenge. But he is generally a patient man, and he can wait for many years.

Iraqi appeals to the Saudis run the gamut from abject flattery, to solemn promises that Iraq never intended to attack the kingdom in 1990, to ominous threats and abusive rhetoric.[9] Iraqi spokesmen occasionally call for "Arab reconciliation"—essentially codewords for Saudi Arabia and Kuwait to forgive and forget.[10] More often, however, Iraqi spokesmen deliver *ad hominem* attacks on King Fahd and the royal family and warn Riyadh that the United States is "milking" them.[11] Iraq frequently threatens and insults the kingdom in other ways. For example, in a statement in May 1994, Iraqi foreign minister Muhammad Sa'id al-Sahhaf refused to call the country "Saudi Arabia," and instead insisted on using the geographical terms "Najd" and "Hijaz" (a common practice among Middle Eastern states that do not recognize the legitimacy of the Al-Sa'ud):

> It is well known to the population of Najd and Hijaz and all Arabs and Muslims that the feeble-minded Fahd begins his day by gulping alcoholic drinks just as greedily as beasts guzzle stagnant water, a habit he practices even during the pilgrimages. He is scarcely sober enough to conduct a meaningful conversation . . . his utterings are typically absurd, revolting and hollow. . . . [The Saudi Royal family has served] as an agent of U.S. imperialism since it was brought to occupy Najd and Hijaz in suspect circumstances.[12]

Probably the most offensive accusation in the Iraqi arsenal is the claim that the House of Sa'ud is "of Jewish lineage and spirit," and that their Jewish ancestors collaborated with Persian Zorastrians "to stab the Caliph al-Faruq"[13] ('Umar Bin al-Khattab, the Second Caliph). In a commentary on an important speech by Saddam Husayn on Revolution Day 1994, a well-known Iraqi journalist warned Saudi Arabia and its allies:

> No one in the region or the world . . . can ignore Iraq and its role in its environment if he wants security and stability for himself and his interests, now or in the future. Therefore, the regimes targeted by the Iraqi call are asked to ponder carefully their hostile policies against Iraq and avoid the . . . reactions that only harmed them . . . and . . . might take place if the hostile stands against Iraq continue.[14]

Given Baghdad's ham-handed efforts to court Riyadh, it is no surprise that the Saudis have generally had little desire to reconsider their overall position toward Iraq in the years since the war. During the crises of November 1997 and January–February 1998, the Saudi press generally was extremely critical of Saddam Husayn and blamed him for all the suffering of the Iraqi people as well as for the consequences of his stubborn obstruction of the activities of the UN Special Commission (UNSCOM) in Iraq. The commander of Arab forces during the Gulf War, Saudi Lt. Gen. Prince Khalid Bin Sultan ibn 'Abd al-'Aziz, exclaimed, "as long as Saddam remains in power the threat [to Gulf security] will remain."[15] Similarly, 'Ukkaz wrote, "The Iraqi regime is certainly responsible for all the measures taken to stop its irresponsible responses to [UN Security Council] resolutions," and it demanded that Iraq comply fully with all of the relevant UN Security Council resolutions.[16] Following his meeting with Secretary of State Madeleine Albright in early February 1998, Crown Prince 'Abd Allah ibn 'Abd al-'Aziz issued a communiqué castigating the Iraqi regime for its obstructiveness:

> The two sides agreed on the need for the Baghdad government to comply unconditionally with the will of the international community. . . . [The two sides favor] exhausting all diplomatic means . . . because the failure of these means will lead to dire consequences which the Iraqi regime will bear if it insists on continuing to refuse to comply fully.[17]

By implication, then, both the Saudi press and the government legitimized a military campaign in the event that Iraq did not change its position, and they laid the blame for any such campaign on Saddam.

Nevertheless, recent shifts in the politics of the Gulf have caused the Saudis to rethink several Iraq-related positions. First, Riyadh is unsure of America's readiness actually to overthrow Saddam or its ability to contain him over the long term. After seven years with no end to Saddam in sight, some among the Saudi power elite feel that their country should hedge its bets. The country has always balanced its close relations with the United States by staying on good terms with major Arab states. During and after the Gulf War its reliance on the United States became particularly heavy, but the kingdom is now moving back to its traditional position at the heart of Arab consensus and, as a result, it is slowly and almost imperceptibly shifting toward a more lenient approach to Saddam's Iraq. Second, Arab resentment at the stagnation in the Arab–Israeli peace process—as well as the growing intimacy between Israel and Turkey—are adding to the pressure Riyadh feels to realign its own position on Iraq with that of the Arab majority. Last, the Islamist opposition in Saudi Arabia has always objected to the U.S. presence there and although the Saudi regime seems stable, the royal family prefers not to open itself up to the charges of its domestic opposition.

These pressures have begun to manifest themselves in Saudi behavior. During the September 1996 Irbil crisis, Riyadh reportedly turned down a U.S. request to use Saudi bases to launch attacks on Iraqi targets.[18] It seems that the Saudis concluded that if they were to help prevent Saddam from reimposing control over Iraqi Kurdistan they would stir considerable dis-content at home—discontent they were unwilling to endure in the name of preventing an Arab ruler from regaining control over an area populated by an obstreperous non-Arab minority. In late 1997 and early 1998, impor-tant voices could be heard in the kingdom calling for a somewhat more lenient stance toward Iraq and opposing a military strike. Some suggested that a military operation would only strengthen Saddam.[19] Others claimed that the United States hoped to perpetuate Saddam's rule in Iraq because this justified the U.S. military presence in the Gulf, which ultimately was designed to force Iraq to make peace with Israel and to fragment Iraq.[20] Still other Saudi journalists echoed more general Arab sentiments that airstrikes would harm not Saddam, but the Iraqi people, who had suffered enough from the sanctions.[21]

There have been no calls for normalization with Iraq either from Saudi officials or journalists, and the Saudi view of Saddam and his regime is as uniform as it is dismal. Yet, at the December 1997 Gulf Cooperation Council (GCC) Summit, Crown Prince 'Abd Allah declared, "We the nations of the Gulf have no comfortable place today unless we overcome the past with its events and pains. . . . [The Summit should tackle] sensitive and critical [developments] with insight which is not built on isolationist concepts or leaning toward it."[22] GCC diplomats were at a loss when they tried to interpret these enigmatic sentences. Some believed the prince's words were directed at the GCC states, whereas others saw it as a call to mend GCC fences with Iraq. For its part, the Iraqi Revolutionary Command Council (RCC) described the prince's declaration as "positive," noting, "The RCC wishes to see these statements lead to a new Arab diplomacy, in particular a new diplomacy among Gulf states . . . in order to put a stop to the negative situation prevailing between some Arab countries."[23]

Indeed, the crown prince's cryptic pronouncement may have encouraged the United Arab Emirates to broach the issue of rehabilitating Iraq at the GCC summit, an idea the UAE had quietly been promoting for some time beforehand. At the summit, Shaykh Zayd Bin Sultan Aal Nahyan, president of the UAE, tabled the notion of sending a GCC delegation to Iraq to press Saddam to implement the UN resolutions. Only a few days before, Shaykh Zayd had called for the lifting of sanctions on Iraq. Significantly, during the summit, Prince 'Abd Allah met twice with Shaykh Zayd.[24]

Ultimately, whatever the crown prince may have meant, the Saudi government quickly quashed any suspicions that Riyadh might be ready for a rapprochement with Iraq. A few days after the summit, Saudi newspaper *al-Riyadh* came out with a ferocious denial. It noted that many Arabs had charged Saudi Arabia (or the Gulf States) with responsibility for the suffering of the Iraqi people and responded:

> These self-appointed custodians [of Arabism] would like us to mend our fences with Iraq and shed tears over the plight of its beseiged people. They go on to promote a removal of the sanctions and remind us that the people of Iraq are as much Muslims and Arabs as we are, so why not reach out to them . . . as they struggle with the scourges of a blockade, poverty, disease . . . and [ill] health. They make it sound as if the responsibility for the hungry and widowed women, or orphaned children, . . . rightly lies at our doorstep. . . . Those who would like for us to apologize to Saddam Husayn because we have not let him rape our land are trashing our legitimacy and being extremely stupid. Those who think that there has been a shift in the GCC policies and that the Gulf states are now following a softer line toward Saddam Husayn must understand that there has been no such change."[25]

The Saudis undoubtedly remain extremely wary of Saddam and his regime. This fear induced them to urge the United States to support the Shi'i intifada against Saddam after the Gulf War, even though they had strong reservations about the Shi'a as well. Ultimately, they considered Saddam far more dangerous.[26] Similarly, there is no indication that Saudi Arabia is reconsidering its position vis-à-vis the embargo or the implementation of Resolution 687. The Saudis are committed to the territorial integrity of Iraq, but they blame Saddam for all the tribulations that befell his country. The suffering of the Iraqi people, they feel, should be alleviated by implementing Resolution 986 rather than by lifting the embargo).[27] This attitude has not changed, but the Arab and international circumstances are changing, and the end of Saddam Husayn's rule in Baghdad is not yet in sight.

NOTES

1   See, for example, *al-Thawra*, August 3, 1997, in *Agence France Presse (AFP)*, August 3, 1997; Nuri Marsumi, *al-'Iraq*, August 2, 1997, in *Foreign Broadcast Information Service–Near East and South Asia–Daily Report (FBIS-NES-DR)*, August 6, 1997.

2   See *al-Jumhuriyya*, August 2, 1994, in *FBIS-NES-DR JN0708200094*, August 8, 1994, pp. 44–45.

3   Iraqi vice president Taha Yasin Ramadan was reported to have said to reporters in Baghdad that the new border has "no judicial value"; see *AFP*, June 7, 1998. He later denied that he had said it, but his denial still implied nonrecognition of the borders; see *Middle East News Agency (MENA)*, June 7, 1998.

4   See, for example, the comments of the Kuwaiti government, in a statement for the seventh anniversary of the invasion, *Kuwait News Agency (KUNA)*, August 3, 1997, in *AFP*, August 3, 1997; *Radio Kuwait*, August 29, 1997, in *FBIS-NES-DR*, August 29, 1997.

5   See *al-Khalij*, February 2, 1996, in *al-Malaff al-'Iraqi*, no. 51 (March 1996), p. 33.

6   See *AFP*, August 2, 1997, reporting on supportive articles in *al-Qabas* and *al-Ra'y al-'Amm*, and on the objection on the part of *al-Anba*.

7   See *Xinhua News Agency*, August 18, 1997, on the futile twenty-fifth monthly meeting of the Kuwaiti–Saudi–Iraqi–American–British–French committee assigned to resolve this issue.

8   There are signs of a visit by Dr. Ahmad Chalabi, head of the Iraq National Congress (INC), to Kuwait. See *Radio Kuwait*, July 31, 1997, in *FBIS-NES-DR*, July 31, 1997.

9   For example, see the Ministry of Information and Culture to the *Iraqi News*

Agency (INA), February 3, 1994, in *FBIS-NES-DR,* February 4, 1994, p. 22.

10 See, for example, Mazhar 'Arif, chief editor of *al-Rafidayn* magazine, writing in *Babil,* November 22, 1997.

11 Sabri Hammadi, *al-Thawra,* June 20, 1994; see also *al-Thawra,* August 4, 1994.

12 Foreign Minister Sahhaf on *Iraq Radio Network,* May 26, 1994, in *FBIS-NES-DR JN2605195694* ("Foreign Minister Assails 'Feeble-Minded' King Fahd"), May 26, 1994, p. 34; see also *al-Jumhuriyya,* May 28, 1994; *al-Thawra,* May 29, 1994.

13 See the comments of Shaykh 'Ali al-'Ujayli, in *al-Thawra,* February 4, 1994.

14 *Babil,* July 21, 1994.

15 *'Ukkaz,* January 2, 1998, in *FBIS-NES-DR JN1701211098,* January 17, 1998.

16 *'Ukkaz,* October 24, 1997, in *FBIS-NES-DR JN 2710171597,* October 27, 1997.

17 *Saudi Arabian Television Network,* February 2, 1998 in *FBIS-NES-DR LD0202202898,* February 2, 1998.

18 *Washington Times,* September 4, 1996.

19 Editorial, *al-Riyadh,* November 17, 1997, in *FBIS-NES-DR JN2611211597,* November 26, 1997.

20 See *al-Jazira,* November 25, 1997, in *FBIS-NES-DR JN0212214797,* December 2, 1997.

21 See *al-Riyadh,* November 21, 1997, in *FBIS-NES-DR JN2511192397,* November 25, 1997; editorial, *al-Riyadh,* November 28, 1997, in *FBIS-NES-DR JN0312204597,* December 3, 1997; *al-Jazira,* February 1, 1998, in *FBIS-NES-DR JN0102123098,* February 1, 1998.

22 *Jordan Times,* December 24, 1997.

23 Ibid.

24 Ibid.; see also *Jordan Times,* December 15, 1997, and *al-Hayat,* December 22, 1997.

25 See *al-Riyadh,* December 29, 1997, in *FBIS-NES-DR JN0501123098,* January 5, 1998.

26 Author conversation with a senior U.S. administration official who was in Saudi Arabia at the time of Iraq's Shi'i intifada; Washington, D.C., May 18, 1998.

27 Defense Minister Sultan ibn Abd al-Aziz, quoted in *al-Sharq al-Awsat,* September 16, 1997, p. 4, in *FBIS-NES-DR,* September 16, 1997.

Chapter 10

Conclusions

Saddam Husayn's position within Iraq is certainly much weaker today than it was on the eve of the Gulf War. The repeated crises in his extended family have greatly reduced the president's willingness to trust many of his closest relatives, his relations with key elements of his al-Bu Nasir tribe are similarly strained, and responses to tribally based coup plots since 1990 have alienated him from parts of three of the most powerful Sunni Arab tribes—the Jubbur, the ʿUbayd, and the Dulaym. The army is disheartened and frustrated, and even in the Republican Guard and Special Republican Guard there are budding pockets of disaffection.

This is not to suggest that Saddam's regime is in imminent danger of falling. Saddam retains many devoted followers and a terrifying internal security apparatus, including *al-Amn al-Khass* (the Special Security Organization [SSO]) and the *Himaya* (Palace Guard)—two bodies in which no meaningful disaffection has thus far been exposed. Most of the Special Republican Guard, the Republican Guard, and the intelligence services also remain loyal. The opposition, moreover, remains disunited and relatively marginalized. Disgruntled elements are unable to revolt because they lack the ammunition and heavy armament to take on Saddam's Special Republican Guard, SSO, and palace guards. The secular–expatriate opposition, in the form of the liberal Iraq National Congress (INC), is now regrouping, but this process will require time and support; its base in Kurdistan once challenged the regime by gathering information and transmitting propaganda to Baghdad, thus threatening Saddam's legitimacy, but the 1996 attack on Irbil wiped out much of the INC's infrastructure. Similarly, Shiʿi insurgents, especially those connected with the Tehran-based

147

Supreme Assembly of the Islamic Revolution in Iraq (SAIRI), are active in the South, but Iranian support for them is limited. Without massive external help, neither the INC nor the SAIRI can expect to threaten the regime seriously. A popular revolt against the regime along the lines of the Iranian revolution in 1978–1979 or the Iraqi *intifada* (uprising) of 1991 does not seem very likely, for the simple reason that, after nearly thirty years of Saddam's terror and after at least 30,000 casualities during the intifada, the population has been cowed and Saddam has made sure that their minimum requirements are met.

Nevertheless, Saddam's power base—the people and institutions on which he relies to keep himself in power—has narrowed considerably over the last three years, and this has had important ramifications for Iraqi policy. Since late 1994, internal problems have helped to push the regime into a series of unpalatable or risky moves. In October 1994, for example, fear of domestic unrest apparently led Saddam to order his troops once again to "march on Kuwait." The total devastation of the local currency then forced Saddam to accept United Nations Security Council Resolution 986, thus diminishing the prospect of either a popular revolt or the complete disintegration of social order. It also enabled Saddam to increase the perks for his close supporters. The sudden proliferation of dangerous coup plots among his Republican Guards strongly influenced Saddam's decision to attack Kurdish-held Irbil in 1996, thus risking a confrontation with the United States. Finally, popular frustration with sanctions-induced deprivations and suspicions among the elite that the oil embargo would never end and that their leader had condemned Iraq to eternal subservience seem to have led Saddam to challenge the UN weapons inspections and sanctions regime at a time when he saw a window of opportunity in the UN Security Council, in 1997.

Remarkably, Saddam has found in dramatic foreign policy gestures at least temporary relief from his domestic problems. Accepting Resolution 986 alleviated the sense of desperation among the Iraqi people—a desperation that had been caused as much by Saddam's callousness as by the sanctions themselves. The successful attack on Irbil restored the Guards' pride and confidence in their leader. His challenges to the UN Special Commission (UNSCOM) and the United States created the impression (among Iraqis) of movement on inspections and sanctions by placing UNSCOM under growing pressure in the UN Security Council to reveal information that, ironically, could help Iraq deceive the inspectors. A new atmosphere of mistrust forced UNSCOM inspectors to spend much of their energy and time on proving every point in the UN Security Council, rather than on inspecting Iraqi sites.[1] In addition, whenever it does not like UNSCOM's modus operandi, Iraq now can turn to the UN secretary-general and his representative in Baghdad. This places new restrictions on UNSCOM. Hampering the inspections regime, then, has greatly enhanced confidence and optimism among Saddam's elite.[2] Most important of all, these actions have apparently restored Iraq's diplomatic stature, with senior diplomats and the UN secretary general frequenting Baghdad as they had done in 1990–1991, and with Arab leaders communicating with Saddam almost as they did during the Kuwait crisis.[3] In short, Iraq seems to be back in the mainstream of world diplomacy.

Moreover, there is every indication that Saddam will continue to pursue this course and real reason to believe he will continue to enjoy success. Although his domestic problems are serious, they do not pose an immediate threat. It will take considerable time before Saddam's security apparatus has eroded to the point at which he is in serious jeopardy, and various initiatives have—at least temporarily—taken the momentum out of several of his most dangerous concerns. Meanwhile, he is scoring international victories at a much more rapid pace, primarily because the Gulf War coalition is falling apart: France, Russia, and China now back Iraq against the United States and Britain; Syria explicitly demands an end to the oil embargo, and Egypt implies such an expectation.[4] There is also a growing tendency in the Arab world to rehabilitate Iraq by, for example, inviting it to participate in the next Arab summit. Finally, Jordan, Syria, and Turkey are now competing for shares in the Iraqi market. In the race between the disintegration of Saddam's regime and the disintegration of the international coalition containing him, the latter is well in the lead. Yet, the stronger Saddam is internationally, the less he will need to face these internal problems. Usually, there is an inverse relationship between the urge to hatch a coup d'état against a dictator, and that dictator's perceived success.

The Meaning of Victory and Defeat for Saddam Husayn

Despite obvious and profound differences between Iraq and the democratic West, the success or failure of foreign policy initiatives is not judged very differently in Baghdad than it is in the United States and other democracies. For Saddam, although foreign exploits have value in themselves, "success" means in the first place accomplishing something that strengthens his domestic position. Sometimes this must be done at the expense of his international relations. Iraq was much weaker internationally after the October 1994 "march" on Kuwait, but the move bought Saddam a few months of calm domestically. Iraq was stronger among its Arab neighbors but weaker internationally after the August 1996 attack on Irbil—an action that could have prevented the lifting of sanctions for months afterward—but it was still a major victory for Saddam: By taking Irbil, he restored the pride of the Republican Guard, shattered the Kurdish opposition, drove the INC from the North, and partially reasserted the role of the central government in northern Iraq. Finally, when he initiated the October–November 1997 crisis, Saddam could not be sure of victory or even limited success. He gambled on a divided UN Security Council and won, but he was apparently ready to pay a price internationally to demonstrate to his power base that the embargo would not be forgotten.

No power in the world can prevent Saddam from declaring victory even after the most devastating defeat: He did so even in 1991, despite having lost Kuwait and much of his armed forces and despite having signed a cease-fire agreement that allowed long-term breach of Iraq's sovereignty by the United Nations. Nevertheless, to convince his power base, Saddam has to provide some proof of his victory. Therefore, even if the West can rightly claim that it achieved meaningful results on its own terms, if Saddam can *convincingly* do the same, it is the West that is the loser. Whenever Saddam's supporters have tallied his gains and losses from any crisis and concluded that he gained from the experience, he has been emboldened to challenge the West once more—and soon.

Thus, Saddam has his power base well under control for the moment, but this does not mean he feels no pressure to deliver an end to the embargo, retain his WMDs, and avoid a major Western military campaign against Iraq. The Iraqi people and Saddam's power base are not always convinced of his "victories"; this is evident from Saddam's many attempts to prove to his officers that Iraq was ready for war—which would thus counter the notion that the Gulf War was a poorly calculated disaster. Likewise, his court ideologues continue to try to answer a common question: Why did Iraq not withdraw from Kuwait peacefully?[5] Saddam's internal problems are therefore a Sword of Damocles hanging over his head. With every new difficulty—every time another family member falls afoul of him, every time another coup plot is discovered among the Republican Guard, every time another tribal body feuds with the president, and every time Iraq's hope for an end to the embargo is dashed, the rope holding that sword frays a bit.

Moreover, Saddam has demonstrated throughout his thirty years in power that he is extremely sensitive to internal threats. If an outside observer would consider a domestic Iraqi problem as having no more than a one percent chance of resulting in a successful coup, Saddam invariably would view this problem as involving an unacceptable risk. As far as internal security is concerned, therefore, Saddam has never taken any chances. He pushes hard to show his supporters the "light at the end of the [embargo] tunnel" and thus to remove the domestic threat looming over his rule. At the same time, however, he must try to avoid a Western military blow; such a blow, if massive enough, would involve a three-fold risk. First, a chaotic situation—such as if the capital city were under a blackout, most communication systems were out of order, and distant explosions could be heard in the city—would be an ideal opportunity for a coup d'état. Second, the Shi'is of Saddam's City (a poor quarter of Baghdad with some 1.5 million inhabitants), and even more so those in southern Iraq, may again see in a U.S. attack on Saddam's power base an opportunity to rise in revolt. The possibility is remote, but Saddam cannot ignore it. Finally, even barring these events, if the damage to Saddam's power base is massive, this could erode the support of the same people whose loyalty he is trying to retain.

Finally, Saddam must keep the French and Russians on his side. The combination of a breach with them and a heavy American air campaign is unacceptable to him because it might leave him badly bruised both militarily and politically. Without France and Russia, most Arabs too may forsake him. But—with some important exceptions—Saddam Husayn is *generally* a patient man. Since 1991, when things have gotten tough, he has withdrawn and waited for a new opportunity to present itself. As he apparently sees it, the risk of a massive U.S. air attack, combined with French and Russian acquiesence, is far worse than another delay in the lifting of the embargo.

IS THERE A PATTERN TO IRAQ'S CHALLENGES TO THE UN?

It should be clear that not all the decisions made in Baghdad since the establishment of UNSCOM in April 1991 can be explained rationally. In some cases, apparently, Saddam Husayn simply became angry, frustrated, and impatient. All the same, however, one can see that an important pattern of Iraqi behavior has emerged over the last seven years. Iraq constantly challenges the UN inspection and sanctions regimes with low-level obstructions. Iraqi personnel delay and harass UN inspectors in Iraq. Baghdad is constantly looking for ways to break the sanctions or to complicate the job of enforcing them—such as by flying pilgrims to Saudi Arabia for the Hajj in defiance of the no-fly zones and the UN flight bans. Yet, from time to time, Iraq also mounts major challenges, high-profile obstructions that threaten to undermine key elements of the UN inspection and sanctions regimes. In October 1994 Iraq threatened a new invasion of Kuwait; in 1995 it threatened to end the inspection regime; in 1996 it challenged the Kurdish "sanctuary"; and in 1997 it again threatened the inspection regime.

The frequency of Iraq's major challenges has increased considerably over the last few years, apparently reflecting two important trends in Saddam Husayn's thinking. First, as noted above, his growing domestic problems are putting real pressure on him to find a way out of Iraq's current unpleasant position or at least to demonstrate that he has not given up. Consequently, he resorts to major challenges as a way of accelerating the process or possibly even "resolving" it with a series of blows. Second, Iraqis appear to have learned that the UN, and the United States in particular, can be forced to make concessions through a policy of brinkmanship.

Saddam apparently concluded that his low-level obstructions are useful in helping him both to hang on to his WMDs and to buy a little breathing space from the suffocating sanctions. Yet, they clearly were not putting enough pressure on the UN or the United States to force them to consider actually reining in UNSCOM or ending the sanctions and inspections. By contrast, major challenges did at times bring real results, while costing him relatively little. Saddam gained nothing from his October 1994 move against Kuwait except the humiliation of having to recognize the border with Kuwait and pull back the Republican Guard. This almost certainly taught him that acting in a blatantly aggressive fashion only plays into the hands of the United States, and that it is better to play the aggrieved victim—as he began doing in the autumn of 1997—to garner international sympathy. He also gained nothing in 1995, but he can blame that defeat on Husayn Kamil's defection. In 1996, however, Saddam suddenly made real gains—on his own terms. He split the Kurdish factions, reasserted some of his influence in the North, and by smashing the nascent INC organization demonstrated that there was no viable opposition to his rule.

Iraq's 1997 challenge was even more rewarding. For the first time, Iraq became a participant in UN negotiations. Prior to that autumn, Iraq had merely been an object in UN deliberations; suddenly it was virutally an equal partner. Russian, French, UN, and other officials were once again jetting to Baghdad to find out what Saddam considered an acceptable solution to the impasse. The UN no longer treated Iraq as a vanquished state and a criminal regime that was simply expected to obey the dictates of the international community. Instead, Iraq was again a sovereign state with rights and objectives that the UN had to respect. Of equal importance, Baghdad got many members of the UN to begin discussing the need to give Iraq incentives to cooperate—even to show the Iraqis the "light at the end of the tunnel" that Saddam desperately needed. Even some American voices began to call for a limit on sanctions.

Indeed, by 1997, Western public opinion seemed to be coming around to Saddam Husayn's side. Saddam's propaganda machine has expertly focused the international community on the plight of the Iraqis, predominantly in the Shi'i areas—even though their suffering was caused by Saddam's intransigence and deliberate policies. It is widely recognized that the many who suffer in Iraq are Saddam's helpless hostages, but this does not make their suffering any easier, and it instead focuses Western public opinion and pressure on the sanctions regime. Iraqis, too, are increasingly likely to blame the West for ignoring their plight, rather than Saddam for causing their problems. The oil-for-food arrangements of Resolution 986, and Resolution 1153, while a step in the right direction, have not solved the problem; by early 1998 it emerged that, whereas the food situation improved, Iraqis are suffering most from lack of medicines and hygiene. Purified water, sewage treatment, and having electricity twenty-four hours a day are the population's main concerns, because long electricity breakdowns, sewage flooding neighborhoods, polluted water, and unprocessed sewage dumped into the river are the main causes of disease. The international community must address these issues, or at least prove unequivocally to Iraqis that it is their leader who has deliberately obstructed any improvements.

This change constitutes a major achievement for Saddam Husayn. Although it is unclear at this point whether he will be able to use these footholds to lead Iraq out of the sanctions regime, all indications suggest that maintaining the integrity of the sanctions and inspections regimes will become an increasingly difficult task for those countries that adopt a hard line toward Saddam and his WMDs: the United States, Britain, Kuwait, Saudi Arabia, and others. On the other hand, the changing atmosphere gives Saddam a juicy bone to throw to his power base. He can use Iraq's new-found importance and the international calls for an end to the sanctions to convince the Iraqi elite that he had been correct all along and that his strategy is now bearing fruit. There can be little doubt that this will give him a meaningful boost domestically.

Finally, Saddam has always been attuned to Arab opinions. In many cases he has misjudged their significance, but he has always listened carefully and acted in a way that he believes will enable him and his regime to benefit from developments in the Arab world. He believed, for example, that he could win pan-Arab support after his August 1990 order to invade Kuwait by championing the Palestinian cause against Israel. He was wrong. Arab frustration with the then-new Likud government in Israel was indeed mounting, but few Arab governments were willing to support the expansionist designs of the Iraqi president. In 1996–1997, however, renewed Arab frustration over the slow pace of the peace process served him much better. Arab intellectuals, journalists, diplomats, and politicians started accusing the United States and Britain of "double standards" for applying pressure to Iraq to comply with UN Security Council resolutions but sparing Israel under Prime Minister Binyamin Netanyahu. Regardless of whether one views the "double standard" argument as valid, it became a popular and powerful one in the Arab world, and Saddam Husayn was quick to take advantage of it.

In other words, Saddam Husayn and his regime have undergone a remarkable transformation since mid-to-late 1995, when Saddam was widely perceived in Baghdad as being close to losing power. At that time, his economy was on the brink of collapse and his people utterly demoralized because of his stubborn refusal to accept Resolution 986. He faced bloody infighting among his closest family members and dissension among several of the most important Sunni tribes. Husayn Kamil's defection and panicked admissions to UNSCOM—which thoroughly soured UNSCOM ambassador Rolf Ekeus on Iraqi claims of cooperation and finally convinced Jordan to break with Iraq and side with the United States—seemed to be the nail in Saddam's coffin. Indeed, in June 1996, officers in the Republican and Special Republican Guards prepared a coup d'état.

Today, however, Saddam seems firmly in control in Iraq. He has pacified his family and bought time with the tribes, restored some of the Republican Guard's shattered pride, and convinced his power base that his leadership is effective and is succeeding in having the sanctions and inpsections lifted without having to give up Iraq's WMD arsenal. What is most remarkable about this reversal of fortune, in addition to its quick pace, is its source: the distant international community—European, Asian, and even many Arab states. Indeed, Saddam may be reminded of the forgotten lessons of the Iraq–Iran War: that the international community can serve as something of a counterweight to defuse dangerous internal threats. In short, the international community can also become a part of his power base.

As long as he and his regime rule in Baghdad there is very little hope that Iraq will comply with UN Security Council resolutions, whether in regard to Iraq's WMDs, Kuwaiti prisoners, or human rights. Moreover, the world community should not be surprised to see itself further manipulated to suit Saddam Husayn's purposes. The Iraqi leader, for personal and domestic considerations, has occasionally created crises that badly affect Iraq's foreign relations, but since 1997 these relations have been improving. Nevertheless, if past practices may serve as indicators, then when he feels frustrated and desperate, or victorious and confident, Saddam Husayn might try again to destabilize the Gulf area and, possibly, the Middle East as a whole.

NOTES

1   For UNSCOM's concession, see the report of an agreement signed in Baghdad between Iraqi vice president Tariq 'Aziz and UNSCOM chief Richard Butler, *Agence France Presse (AFP)*, June 14, 1998. The agreement has not been published, but Butler admitted that it imposed "a very significant new workload" on his organization. Iraq, for its part, agreed to some demands but refused to add any information on VX or biological weapons, as they are its most potent weapons of mass destruction; see Barbara Crasette, *New York Times*, June 19, 1998, and Dominic Evans, *Reuters*, June 15, 1998. For a report on the pressure newly applied to UNSCOM at the UN Security Council, see *New York Times*, June 1, 1998. Also based on author's interviews with UN officials, June 1998.

2   Interviews with UN officials, June 1998. Reportedly, in their June 1998 meeting with Butler, 'Aziz and his colleagues were more confident and optimistic than before over the early end of sanctions, even though they still declined to provide Butler all that he requested.

3   For example, Tariq 'Aziz in Syria, Jordan, and Cairo, *Mideast Mirror*, November 24, 1997. See also Issam Hamza, *Reuters*, November 22, 1997.

4   See, for example, Foreign Minister 'Amr Moussa, *Middle East News Agency (MENA)*, April 18, 1998.

5   See, for example, Salah Muktar, editor in chief, in *al-Jamhuriyya*, on November 17, 1993, and January 5, 1994.